WHY BUDDHA SMILES

JØRGEN BISCH

Why Buddha Smiles

TRANSLATED BY

GWYNNE VEVERS

Collins

ST JAMES'S PLACE LONDON

1964

Contents

Colour Plates

COLOUR PLATES

Foreword

Why Buddha Smiles is a book about a journey to Burma, Thailand and Cambodia. In writing about the peoples of these countries I have tried to understand their spiritual background, but I little realised how much I myself would become involved in Buddhism.

Naturally this book does not attempt a complete evaluation of Buddhism—this would need a lifetime's study. It does, however, seek to give, together with my other experiences on the journey, an account of my own personal impressions of Buddhism, acquired during my travels in the East and from the books I have read on the subject.

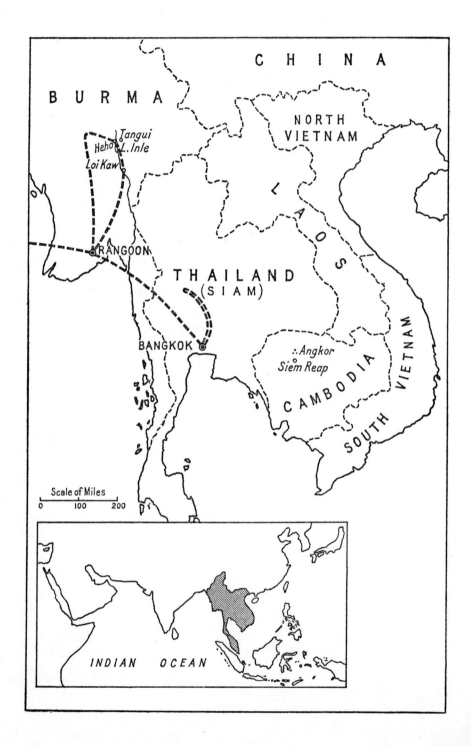

CHINA

BURMA

NORTH
VIETNAM

Tangui
Heho° *L. Inle*

Loi Kaw

L

A

O

S

RANGOON

THAILAND
(SIAM)

BANGKOK

.·. *Angkor*
Siem Reap

CAMBODIA

SOUTH VIETNAM

Scale of Miles
0   100   200

INDIAN OCEAN

CHAPTER I

In Search of the Giraffe Women

"THE WOMEN'S NECKS are encircled by a number of copper rings, so that they become three to four times as long as a normal neck; this is done as a protection against tiger bites."

The man who told me this was perfectly sober. We were sitting in the garden of the famous Raffles Hotel in Singapore, drinking tea in the shade of the tall palm trees.

"It sounds unbelievable," I said. "But tell me more."

"These people are known as Padaungs, and they live in the uncivilised border state of Kayah in Burma—I myself am Burmese, so I know all about it," he replied, a little reproachfully.

"You must excuse me! I certainly believe what you say. In fact I think I have read about these women somewhere. But it sounds fantastic."

"The Padaungs are very warlike; up to a few years ago they were head-hunters—my uncle was killed by them," he continued. "However it is only the women who wear rings round their necks. When a woman has the rings removed, she must have a friend nearby to hold up her head, otherwise she will die. They are known as giraffe women."

"Giraffe women! Tell me where I can find them." I must have already had a new expedition in mind, for we hear and read very little about these remarkable ladies.

"You travel north-north-east from Rangoon for about 600 miles, to the state of Kayah, which is close to the frontier of Thailand. But I don't advise you to try. There are nearly always disturbances, and there is no guarantee that you will meet the giraffe women, for they are nomads. And also they're very shy and refuse to be photographed."

But I had already made my decision; perhaps the fact that they were difficult to meet made it even more exciting to try and find them.

A couple of days later I was back in Denmark to begin my preparations. Little did I expect that this journey would give me even more interesting experiences than the sight of the giraffe women.

"Conditions are very disturbed and it would be dangerous to go up there," said the Burmese authorities when I wrote and asked if I could go to the wild state of Kayah. In their reply they said that I could not get permission in advance, but must seek it from the War Ministry on my arrival in Rangoon.

Difficulties and problems always seem greater the farther away you are from them. I have often found this, and so I confidently bought a ticket from Copenhagen to Rangoon.

Nowadays flying is quite different from what it was a couple of years ago; it is much faster and more comfortable—apart from the relatively long stops on the shorter stages. There is far less noise in a jet than in an ordinary propeller machine, no more than the wind blowing past a modern car travelling at about 90 m.p.h.—but we were flying at six times this speed.

We flew at a height of about five to six miles, so high in fact that I could clearly see the curve of the earth's surface, even though the windows were very small; the world was so far below that no detail could be made out. The River Danube looked like a narrow belt in the grey haze over the earth. The Alps stood out more clearly, but you would have needed excellent sight to pick out an ocean liner on the Mediterranean.

At this height the cloud cover looked like an Arctic icefield, and the sky above was a deep dark blue. I knew this clear light and remembered having a comparable view over the cloud layer when some twelve years ago I climbed Kilimanjaro, which is over 19,000 feet high and Africa's highest mountain. Now we were sitting in the comfortable inclined seats in the pressurised cabin, while luncheon was served. I could not help thinking about Kilimanjaro. This jet aircraft could fly four to five times round the earth in the time it took us to reach the top of the mountain. Then I was mountain-sick for eight days on end, vomiting from lack of oxygen and unable to eat. Here an oxygen mask would drop down automatically from the ceiling if the cabin pressure should accidentally fall slightly below normal.

We slept lightly for a few hours—the nights are short when you fly east—and in the morning we landed in Rangoon, the capital of Burma.

The Strand Hotel, the chief hotel of the city, smelt of spilt beer and of the damp frayed green Burma cheroots. With the constant rain and the high humidity it was both damp and oppressively warm. The towels were wet, and the elevator boy worked like a robot. The chief receptionist sat and stared at a newspaper, without reading it. The bartender leant against the counter and gazed vacantly ahead as though stuffed. The three waiters in the restaurant had each parked themselves on a stool in a mood of depression and disgust. The tables seemed to be clothed in shrouds. A page-boy sat half-dead on the lowest step of the stairs, and when I asked for some matches he jerked slightly, got up and came over to me like a sleep-walker.

The matches would not light because they were too damp. Never mind, my cigar was also too damp to light.

The languid youth sank down on to the stairs again.

Rangoon was in hibernation—in the monsoon and a temperature of 95°F.

> "By the old Moulmein Pagoda, lookin' lazy at the sea
> There's a Burma girl a-settin', and I know she thinks o' me,"

Palm trees and temple bells and flying fish ?

No, when the monsoon sets in the picture in Rudyard Kipling's famous lines scarcely fits.

There was a dog lying across the steps that led down to the street. Was it dead? Why had it not been removed? But no, it was only fast asleep.

I strode over the slumbering Cerberus and stepped out into the living world.

Alongside the covered footway three battered taxis sailed past, for a cabby never sleeps. They had been lying in wait like tigers. If I had to be driven I preferred the small jackals, the rickshaw coolies, with their three-wheeled, sidecar cycles, but for the moment I wanted to walk around the streets and get the feel of the place. However before I had been round the hotel block I was in need of the rickshaw boy who had followed me, because the street was a deep muddy stream. I hailed him.

"Sir, you give me five *kyats* one hour!"

"I'll give you five *kyats* for the whole day," I replied.

"No, sir, ten *kyats*."

"No, thanks, you had better let me get off again. I know that the price is three *kyats*, so it's a lot of nonsense your asking five *kyats*. You had better stop here!"

"O.K., sir, I understand. You know the price," he said with a broad grin. There were no hard feelings.

Just as a pilot needs to be retrained when he switches to a new type of aircraft, so the traveller needs a certain retraining when he leaves the harassed and efficient world of Europe for the slow tempo and the tortuous business methods of the Orient. A bicycle with a sidecar, a so-called trishaw, helps this process—your blood pressure slowly falls and down goes the tempo; you are becoming acclimatised.

The coolie stood up on the tricycle pedals with his bare feet. The sinews of his thin legs quivered and the veins stood out. Slowly the vehicle started to move and we drove through the water in the little streets, with every now and again a pedestrian stepping or hopping across as he tried to get from one arcade to the next. For this it's a good idea to go barefoot.

Bit by bit the westerner falls into the tempo of Rangoon.

But when we drove out from a little side street into the main thoroughfare the tempo changed from adagio to presto. No, it would be wrong to use these familiar musical terms to describe this new turmoil which was more like two cats fighting on a piano keyboard.

They drove on the right side of the road, or on the left or down the middle; buses, lorries and taxis. And in and out of this medley darted the three-wheeled Japanese mini-cabs, their drivers reminding me of Japanese suicide pilots.

Pedestrians rushed across the road, as though tired of life. In among this chaos were dogs, rickshaws, coolie porters and country people, who paid even less attention to the traffic regulations than the local inhabitants.

The conductor of this oriental musical was a poor disregarded traffic policeman, waving his arms and legs about. He had a whistle in his mouth, which he blew shrilly every time someone ignored the traffic regulations. And of course blew it incessantly.

A saffron-robed monk wandered slowly along, his gaze fixed five or six steps ahead. It would have been unseemly for him to jump over a puddle or to run. The traffic reverently avoided his path. He was on his way to quite another, and far more peaceful oriental scene—the sublime solitude of his holy monastery.

My tricycle coolie rode into a rather narrow street and quickly brought my thoughts back to worldly things:

"Sir, you would like to change dollars on the black market? You get twice normal price."

"No, I don't want to get involved, and besides I've already changed my money in the hotel."

"You would like a girl, sir? They are young and you can choose fat or thin, fair or dark!"

"No, I want an umbrella," I replied.

The coolie looked at me wondering whether in my language "umbrella" was perhaps a slang word for a certain type of girl.

Burma is the land of umbrellas—never have I seen so many of them at one time. It seemed a bit effeminate to me, so I buttoned up my raincoat. But it was very hot, and soon the inside of my raincoat was also wet, and my hat felt like a warm pudding on my head. So I bought myself an umbrella—the largest I could find. I paid off the rickshaw boy and walked protected through the town.

About ninety-nine per cent of the land around Rangoon is covered with water—the other one per cent consists of the dykes between the paddy-fields, the flooded areas where they grow the wild mountain rice. The whole area looked as though there had been a gigantic inundation, and the rain came down in a steady deluge. But the peasants keep dry under their big umbrella hats or *khamauk*—monstrous creations of plaited fibre and very decorative. And they work naked to the waist, with the loin-cloth, the *loongyi*, rolled up to the knees. They go about their daily tasks quite contentedly, working up the mud of the fields with a wooden plough drawn by big groaning water buffaloes, and planting out their rice at the appropriate time.

The Burmese have their own characteristic attitude to life. A worker earning three *kyats* a day (about eight shillings) is quite satisfied and would not dream of working harder to earn more. Nor has he any interest in saving, for when he becomes old his children will care for him and he is no great burden to them for the old people can still be of some use in such ways as looking after the grandchildren. Besides it is said that the country people only need to work on the average for half an hour a day in order to pay for their food, clothing and a roof over their heads.

A Burmese is quite happy once he has earned enough for his food and his brightly coloured clothes.

Such a lack of ambition may make you shake your head, but when you hear the Burmese laugh and see their happy smiles—and then compare these with the love of money in the western world, with the competition for social prestige, a radio, a television set and other brain-washing machines, and when you think of the mental pressure brought about by the western way of life, of the surliness, bad nerves, high blood pressure, gastric ulcers and heart disease, you may well wonder whether the Burmese, without even a shirt to their backs, are not happier than we are. Perhaps the happiest of all are the young Burmese girls in their bright red *loongyis,* their delicate shoulders covered by fine, semi-transparent silken blouses.

The average Burmese is not interested in business, and so in both large and small towns trade is in the hands of the Chinese and Indians. The Burmese are just not adapted for the effort, the pressure and the speculation which go with a business life.

The Government would like trade to be in the hands of the Burmese, and so there is a law which gives the country's own natives a big advantage in importing goods—but what do they do with these import con-cessions? They sell them to Indians and Chinese, who put their own percentage on the price of the goods—and in the end the Burmese themselves have to pay this too.

A young Burmese girl, who had been a student in London, wrote a little article on life in Burma, and began it by thanking her father and mother, "because in the course of their daily life they have reared their five children to the shining middle path of modera-tion."

"The Americans believe they can buy friendship with money," so say the Burmese. There had naturally been a certain bitterness towards the imperialist British who had ruled the country until 1948, but this is now forgotten; the British are respected.

The Burmese do, however, have a marked distrust of the large nations, and particularly of the Europeans who want to invest money in Burma. "We are a rich country, the land is fertile, and we have both oil and minerals; there is no hurry to exploit these riches, because we have all we need for the time being. There are not many rich people in our country, nor on the other hand need anyone starve, so why should we seek foreign investment?"

Buddha's smile, although enigmatic and sublime, yet gives an impression of clearly understanding the problems of everyday life

They work hard in the paddy-fields until far into the evening. The water buffalo
has its shower-bath just before work ceases

While Burma was under British rule from 1885 to 1948 there was considerable resentment because the country had joint status with India. For Burma, like many small countries, had a fear of being swallowed up by a larger one—in this case India or China. The Burmese is also well aware that he would find it difficult to compete in everyday life against the individual Indian.

Developments have rapidly demonstrated that this fear is well-grounded; the influence of the Indians has been quite catastrophic. For the Burmese has an easy-going disposition. He does not worry much about the practical problems of the morrow—on the whole he does not worry about practical problems at all, unless they are directly forced on him. He loves a good party. At every opportunity, for example a wedding, the admission of a monk or some other religious festival, he is ready to spend, not only every penny he possesses, but also as much as he can borrow, regardless of the extortionate rate of interest charged by the Indians. A few months later, if his affairs are again on a sound footing, he will not hesitate once more to offer his last shilling to pay, for example, for gold-leaf for one of the numerous pagodas.

The Indian, on the other hand, has generations of poverty behind him and centuries of experience in business, and he pinches and scrapes, and it is he who lends out money at impudently high rates, often without security. It is too tempting for the easy-going Burmese—and gradually property passes into the hands of the Indians.

Out in the country this situation often has deplorable consequences. For when the Indians get possession of land, and lease it out for only six or twelve months at a time, nobody is interested in manuring it, and in many places the production from Burmese agricultural land is down to a tenth of what it was a few decades ago.

"Good government cannot replace self-government," said Lord Durham some 120 years ago. But the noble lord was in no way an anti-colonial revolutionary, simply one of the historic personalities of colonialism, who even then was aware that the best colonial government was no substitute for self-government—however confused and inefficient this might be.

They say, as they do in most other former colonies, that in Burma the natives have enormous difficulty in coming to an agreement and in forming even a tolerably effective government in the country, that even to-day they are plagued by bureaucrats on the one side, and by rebels and robber bands on the other. Nevertheless during my long journey

I never once heard anyone express a wish for the British to return to put things in order again.

Even the slow progress made by the careful British colonists has obviously been too fast for the Burmese. Now the British have left the country, and progress has not only come to a halt, but to western eyes has even taken several steps backwards.

But this the Burmese do not appear to regret in the least.

CHAPTER II

Psychological Warfare

"You must ask the Department of Psychological Warfare," said the little smiling man who sat behind an enormous desk in the Burmese Ministry. I nearly burst out laughing.

"*Where*, did you say?"

"The Department of Psychological Warfare," he repeated without blinking, and then wrote down an address and the name of a colonel for me.

The department with the awe-inspiring name was housed in a large building which lay about a twenty-five-shilling taxi ride outside Rangoon.

I did not know whether I should find some kind of Sing-Sing, or an oriental edition of Madame Tussaud's Chamber of Horrors—or a Goebbels-type propaganda centre. Why on earth should I be going there? But of course it is not unusual for writers to be used in psychological warfare.

The building proved to be a radio station to which at least a hundred offices had been attached, and through these I wandered one after the other. It was like a visit to the underworld, or like a nightmare, where one runs from one empty room to another, for all the rooms were empty. There was not a soul about.

It is true that near the entrance hall I did find a porter, after I had spent several minutes tracking him down by the echo of his footsteps, which reverberated through the empty corridors.

He could not speak a word of English and apparently had no desire to help me find Colonel U Ba Tong. All he did was to point to one of the corridors and it was then that I started to roam through this jungle of staircases, passages and side-passages, doorways and offices. They looked as though they had only been deserted a few seconds ago—or perhaps the office workers were just sitting underneath their desks playing hide and seek with me.

Finally I found a little man whom I gripped firmly by the arm—partly to see if he was really alive. I held on to him until I was sure that he had really taken in the name U Ba Tong and had led me to the colonel's office.

The office was empty, but I found a telephone number on a letter heading, and this I noted down.

With this meagre trophy I drove back to the hotel in a tropical rainstorm which was so torrential that the water came up through the floor of the taxi.

When the porter heard of my experience, he quite calmly told me that all offices close for three hours in the middle of the day, but that I would find somone out there later on.

There is continuous guerrilla warfare in Burma, and in some areas you can only drive in convoys, whilst others are only open to the army. So in planning my expedition into the interior of Burma I had to go about it in the official way and try to get the backing of authority. And this is where the psychological warfare came into the picture.

Later in the afternoon I eventually got in touch with a *Captain* U Ba Tong; perhaps it was a psychological warfare trick that the captain had exactly the same name as the colonel. It was through him that all my negotiations were carried out. I never set eyes on the colonel.

At first the authorities gladly put at my disposal a suitable vehicle together with a crew. Then a day before my departure I was told that the offer was a mistake. Finally they rang up an hour later and said that the mistake was a mistake, and that the car and crew would come to my hotel next morning at six a.m.

At five o'clock the following day I was ready with all my gear, and at nine the car came, which should have been there at six. In the car there sat a man called U Maung Maung Kin and his son and his cousin, a driver and his brother-in-law, a reserve driver and two of his friends, as well as the man who was responsible for the vehicle, and his sister and three other persons, who probably just wanted a picnic. After three hours of psychological warfare I managed to get rid of most of them and thus made space for the baggage.

Our reduced crew now consisted only of U Maung Maung Kin, who as he modestly put it, was responsible for my life and food, and his son and two drivers, plus the gentleman who had to make sure that the car got back in good condition, and who was therefore always worried.

So I really had a complete little private army at my disposal, for in fact it was also intended that the five men should act as my bodyguard. Certain parts of the area through which we were to pass were very wild; time after time reports came in of attacks by robbers and of small commando raids carried out by the partisans who roam around continuously in the big jungle areas.

An acquaintance had told me that it was almost impossible to travel nowadays in the interior of Burma. The individual states, in particular the Shan States, were mobilised in order to free themselves from the super-state of Burma, and in addition there were robber bands who plundered as never before. It was considered dangerous for Europeans and even for Burmese wearing European clothes to travel by train.

One was most strongly advised not to go out into the country without a police escort. This all sounded rather over-cautious; the only snag was that the police escort was almost unobtainable.

A short time ago a train on the Mandalay line was held up, and all the Europeans and Burmese in western clothes were taken out and shot. A couple of days after the attack on the Mandalay train the largest Rangoon newspaper reported that a plantation manager who wanted to inspect a teak forest had managed to get hold of an escort of thirty-six armed policemen.

On the following day the paper reported in big headlines:

PLANTATION MANAGER ATTACKED AND KILLED

Then followed details of the murder, and right at the end, for the sake of the record, it was mentioned that the thirty-six policemen had also been killed.

Now it was not that I personally feared such an attack. It might indeed have been an interesting experience—if one got out of it alive— and also there was a certain comfort in the fact that the robbers in Burma very seldom kill those who travel unarmed; they merely seize anything of value they can lay hands on.

U Maung Maung Kin, my unarmed bodyguard and interpreter, proved to be an excellent and conscientious assistant, in fact almost too conscientious. He immediately asked that I should regard him as a liaison officer and not just as an interpreter. He behaved as though he was one of Burma's most trusted men, and took his job of looking after me very seriously.

He stopped at every village along our route and asked whether there had been any recent robber activity. And at each little police post he went in and telephoned to the next post to inquire whether the road was clear.

"Is that not being too cautious?" I asked him.

"No, I am naturally particularly careful, because I am responsible for you, but truly I would also make inquiries if I was travelling alone," he said, and sent a betel-tinted gobbet of spit out of the car window.

I felt that behind all this there was something to do with state security, and that he did not want to go into it. But when a little later on we passed a derailed train, I asked:

"So the revolt has still not been completely subdued?"

"Well, yes, that train has been there for over a year. When I ask whether the road is clear it is first and foremost because I am concerned about the robbers who have obtained arms from the partisans. But there are now no big resistance groups here."

"What has happened to them?" I asked.

"They have made peace with the Government. Burma was once divided up between different tribes, and as a rule the title of chief was passed down from father to son, whether or not the son was fit for the job. This applied particularly in the northern states where the chiefs have held on to their positions. They have carried on bitter guerrilla warfare against the Government, but the fighting has now completely stopped, even though one can still find blown-up bridges and derailed trains."

"How have they managed to pacify the country again?"

"The Government has paid compensation. In the state of Kayah, for example, there were three chiefs, and previously each one had a vote in our Parliament. But in the years prior to 1960 one after another they renounced their official titles as chiefs. The two most important chiefs, Kantarawaddi and Bawlkeh, each got compensation amounting to five lakhs (1 *lakh*= 500,000 *kyats*= £7,500, so each got a total of about £37,500). On the other hand little Kyetpogyi only received one lakh. But now the chiefs of the various states have just broken the agreement and are again mobilising in an attempt to gain their independence from Rangoon," added my liaison officer seriously.

It is paradoxical that a Buddhist should be a soldier, and I was therefore very anxious to hear how they organised their military service.

My first meeting with the military was not pleasant. It took place during our journey to Lake Inle, on a stretch when I myself was at the wheel. I had just overtaken a military vehicle which was creeping along with true oriental composure. A few minutes later we heard an ill-tempered hoot, and before I could react, U Maung Maung Kin grasped the wheel and wrenched the car over to one side. At the same moment the military wagon boomed past—in the middle of the road.

"Whenever a military vehicle appears you must keep in to the side," he explained. "This applies whether the car is coming towards you or approaching from the rear—and it is best not to overtake them because that offends them; then they may drive you into the ditch."

"Surely that's crazy," I replied. "The man who roared past us at top speed should be reported to the police."

"The police have no power over the military. The army is a state within the State, in fact it *is* the state," replied U Maung Maung Kin and shook his head sadly. "You mustn't write about it in your book, and for heaven's sake remember to get out of the way when you see a soldier behind a steering-wheel."

"How can a Buddhist be a soldier?" I asked.

"Well, it can be done," replied U Maung Maung Kin. "Perhaps it would be better to ask how a soldier can be a Buddhist. It's a bit difficult sometimes. Soldiers do not go down on their knees in front of the monks, as the rest of us do, but fortunately there are many good soldiers who enter a monastery when they have got through their military service, as it were to cleanse themselves and revive their ideals."

I had already discovered, when I was referred to the Department of Psychological Warfare, that the military play a prominent rôle in Burma. The army has extended its scope to include many fields of interest; it goes in for trade in a big way and makes things so difficult for foreign firms that it has gradually managed to take over more and more commercial undertakings. Quite recently one of the Danish East Asiatic Company's big concerns was handed over to the Military Trade Department.

The road crossed the flat country on a high dyke, which was surrounded by canals and paddy-fields. The delicate pink lotus flowers shone in the dark waters of the canals. In the fields the rice had been planted out a couple of months before and it now covered almost all the water or swampy soil that it was growing in. But if you looked into the sun the light gleamed and sparkled on the water beneath the rice plants.

Here, where the ground is low-lying, it does not take much for floods to create havoc. In some places the water lay over the road; and in one spot it had washed the road away for a stretch of a quarter of a mile. We linked hands and waded on ahead of the car and found that the water never reached higher than our knees, so the car was able to demonstrate its qualities as an amphibious vehicle.

It is now fashionable for the little herdsmen to wrap themselves up in a brilliantly coloured semi-transparent plastic sheet; when it rains they pull this over their heads instead of using a *khamauk*, which is a hat made of broad wood fibres. When a primitive population abandons its own products and uses modern materials, such as plastic, there is nearly always a loss from the æsthetic viewpoint. But this was not so in the present case. The beautiful red, blue and pale yellow colours which they had chosen looked very gay in the dark-green landscape.

The little herdsmen stood quite still like big iris flowers and let the rain pour down on them, or they moved off after their cattle like flapping butterflies which had been forced to earth by the pouring rain.

In many places the enormous downpours had breached the dykes round the paddy-fields; here and there the fields had been simply washed away. But the Burmese obviously meet misfortune with a smile. They know that nothing is so bad that it benefits no one—they have the chance of a change of diet for the flooded fields swarm with fish. In one place a whole village was out with small nets, walking through the muddy stream, catching fish which were a little larger than sticklebacks.

In another place some boys had already repaired one of the small dykes around the field and were now baling out the water with a tin-can on the end of a long pole. By means of a block and tackle the work could be done with a kind of pendulum movement, which needed little power to keep it going. The water they baled out was allowed to splash down into a basket, which sifted out the small fish; in this way they caught two birds with one stone.

The water buffaloes here looked a little bit like the African buffaloes, but their massive horns and rhino-like bodies made them possibly even more menacing in appearance. In fact they are just as peaceful as European milch cows. When the young herdsmen are tired of wading in the mud they sit up on the back of the leading buffalo, and this gives them a good view over their herd; they only have to be ready to jump off quickly if the buffalo decides to lie down in a mudhole, for a buffalo is very fond of this kind of cosmetic bath. When the animal gets up it often has a half inch layer of mud all over it, and when this dries the black buffalo has become quite a pale grey. But it's still not beautiful.

In the evening the little cowboys drive the buffaloes to a hole with clean water. They splash them with water and then rub and scrub them—a job that is about as comprehensive as washing a muddy lorry. The animals don't seem to mind, in fact they appear to enjoy this treatment. The sun is still hot and the buffaloes then have their evening rest of an hour in another pond, where they lie with their bodies completely submerged in the cool water and with only the nostrils, ears and eyes above the surface.

One evening at about sunset we rushed past one of these waterholes. I stopped, as I thought I had seen a lotus flower in some new rich colour. But when I got back to the waterhole I found that the orange-red "flowers" were in fact the ear openings of a herd of buffaloes, who all lay with their ears turned towards the setting sun, trapping the warm rays with these miniature reflectors. Then I also caught a glimpse of the jet-black eyes and the puffing nostrils.

A young herdsman came running from the opposite side to drive the animals home. He threw a stone into the water behind them. For a moment the red ears turned round towards the sound of the stone hitting the water. It looked as though a row of red lamps had all been turned off at the same time, by the action of a single switch. Then the powerful animals lumbered out of the dark water and went off homewards.

U Maung Maung Kin not only guarded my life, but he also looked after my money; shortly after he had designated himself as liaison officer he asked whether I would entrust him with a sum equivalent to about ten shillings, and it wasn't very long before he got the whole of the money chest made over to him. If he looked after me in an emergency half as well as he looked after my money I had nothing to fear.

A couple of nights in a Government rest-house produced problems I could not have foreseen and led to endless argument about money, even though the bill was accurate in detail.

As a rule it cost six shillings to sleep in a bed, with an extra shilling if there was a blanket. You might also have to pay extra if there was a mattress, but this was really a little private fiddle on the part of the caretaker, for by rights the mattress was included in the price.

Then you had to pay two shillings a head for the use of electric light—but only one shilling where you had to make do with candles—

even though you used just the same amount of light whether there were six people or one in the same room. There was also a special lavatory supplement for each person, and you had to pay extra for water. But my good liaison officer was a very scrupulous manager, and when one morning he found out that only three of his little party had used the lavatory he insisted on a reduction in the price.

The argument was so loud and heated that I was afraid that it might develop into real warfare, of a kind far beyond the purely psychological; it was not the least use my trying to explain to U Maung Maung Kin that I would rather pay the price demanded than waste several hours in talk. He simply refused to listen to me.

After about two hours it seemed that the problem had been settled—with U Maung Maung Kin and the landlord embracing each other—for it appeared that a section of the party had in the meantime used the lavatory.

"Next time you must pay what they ask," I said to U Maung Maung Kin, as we sat down to lunch, "so that we can make an early start."

The good man was so surprised that he almost dropped his chopsticks, and such a pained look spread over his face that I immediately had to comfort him. Then he gave me an hour's lecture on his duty to me and my cash-box and on his honour as an officer. It was only after this that we could get on our way again.

Yes, he was really quite unique. In the evening he asked his men which of them intended to use the new rest-house's lavatory on the following day, and at four o'clock in the morning I awoke to hear him knocking up the landlord and beginning to settle the account on the basis of the advance information he had already gleaned.

That day we really managed to set off at seven o'clock; we had a long and difficult drive with several stops and punctures and were really exhausted when we reached a little village where there was no rest-house and where everything appeared to be closed up.

First the liaison officer made some "official approaches" to the police station, to the mayor's house (where after prolonged banging a woman intimated that her husband had not yet come home and she had no idea where he was), to the deputy mayor's house, where the whole family was away, and then to three or four other addresses, where nobody was willing to give us a night's lodging.

Finally we went back to the police station and asked once more whether they could not help us. The police station was a little two-storied bungalow, to which a little party of police came every half hour to relieve the others. They wore the most varied uniforms. Some sported epaulettes and gold braid and had fine military caps, others arrived with berets and one had a soft felt hat and a knitted pullover. The footwear was also fairly mixed, ranging from boots to canvas shoes or puttees and bare toes. But they were all heavily armed and for several months they had successfully prevented robber bands from attacking the village.

When we again came forward with our request for a night's lodging the duty watch had first to forward our request to a superior. The latter sent a patrol of nine men back to the police station and this posse marched up to the loft of the bungalow where they were to prepare our beds for the night.

In the meantime we sat in the car or walked up and down along the road trying to keep the mosquitoes at bay. The driver had settled himself against a tree for a nap, and by his side was a mongrel dog whose whole body was pink, because it had lost its fur through some form of dermatitis. It was scratching incessantly and when the driver also diligently rubbed himself in his sleep it looked as though they were in competition.

I myself was so tired from sitting doubled up in the car that I lay down on the road and went to sleep. But I was awakened every quarter of an hour by the howling of the hundreds of dogs which lived in the village. Buddhists are not allowed to kill and this accounts for most houses having five or six dogs. But I have no idea why they should all howl at the same time, and at fifteen-minute intervals.

I went to sleep again thinking of Kumbel's jingle: "What's the use of ten men trying to sleep if one dog wants to bark," but here there were hundreds of dogs.

It was two o'clock in the morning when the police woke me to report that they had now cleared the loft for us.

This loft was a big lumber-room. It had certainly never been cleared since the house was built, but now most of the junk had been stowed away at one end of the room, so that at the other end we could spread newspapers and lie down. As guest of honour I had five papers, the others two each.

Breakfast, which we ate at a little Indian restaurant, consisted of a soup which tasted like ignited dynamite. We ate it with china spoons, presumably because metal ones would have immediately dissolved in it.

The meal was soon over, but then came a whole hour of oratorical display, and at one point some early morning gymnastics, before my dear lifeguard and cashier had settled up with the proprietor, who wanted more money for *my* meal because I was a European. Eventually I was charged at the same rate as the Burmese.

In my youth I spent many years studying both general psychology and child psychology, and even some animal psychology, but psychological warfare was a new science to me. I soon gave up trying to follow it and handed over the whole campaign to U Maung Maung Kin.

After we had driven for five days and covered some hundreds of miles, got the better of five rest-house caretakers—psychologically—and two hens and one duck—more militarily than psychologically—as well as injuring the muddy coat of a water buffalo and thereby losing ourselves a front mudguard, we came at last to the final stop before Lake Inle.

In a little coffee shop my guardian angel drew up his balance sheet.

During the journey we had *saved* a total of 27/- by bargaining on the price of various meals, 45/- by haggling over the price of beds, because these had lacked mattresses, and a similar sum because half of my army had relieved themselves in the jungle rather than in the expensive conveniences of the rest-houses.

On the other hand U Maung Maung Kin was not interested in the total *expenses* of the trip, nor indeed in the amount we had in reality lost on the various savings, because as a rule when he had got through the business dealings, he had to produce considerable tips to get the caretakers of the rest-houses into a good humour again.

According to my private calculations we had, during our 120-hour trip, spent fifty hours driving, twenty hours eating and six hours repairing the vehicle. We had slept for about thirty hours and the balance of the time had been spent in—psychological warfare!

CHAPTER III

Lake Inle

THE CAR had struggled over the pass in the lowest gear. It was foggy; water dripped from the dark, comfortless jungle, rippled down the mountainside and made the road even softer. There was no question here of keeping to the right or left; you had to drive as close in as possible to the mountain, because the road was so friable that there was a risk of the outer edge giving way. And many of the ravines were so deep that there would not have been much left of us if the car had fallen over.

After two more sharp bends we were suddenly on the other side of the mountain, with sunshine and a blue sky. Below us opened a landscape on the grand scale—somewhat reminiscent of Switzerland or Uganda. U Maung Maung Kin pointed to a glistening silvery expanse far out towards the horizon.

"Now we've only got about thirty miles to go," he said.

"You're not really telling me that we can see the lake so clearly from a distance of thirty miles?" I asked.

"Yes, you can see it when the sun is against you and the water surface reflects the light. Also, it is thirty miles by road, but much less as the crow flies."

After driving for three to four hours we stopped on the edge of the lake where there was a little village called Yawnghwe. With amazing efficiency U Maung Maung Kin immediately started to secure for us one of the four motor-boats which ply on this 30-mile long lake.

Once we had stowed all the film equipment on board and had got hold of five large umbrellas to protect the cameras against the relentless sun, we set course towards Kyauktaing and others of the so-called floating villages, which are actually built on piles.

No sooner had we started the somewhat obstinate outboard motor than we had to stop it again; we had come face to face with a canoe with only half an inch of freeboard! Another difficult start—and a minute later a second canoe which would have been swamped by our wake, and so it went on. I suppose we must have stopped some twenty times in the course of the first quarter of an hour. For the canoe traffic along the banks was dense, and since the four wretched motor-boat owners were very much in the minority they had to take care not to raise an opposition which could easily have driven them from the lake.

We sailed through a channel which had been cut through the thick mat of luxuriant water hyacinths, tall rushes and other swamp plants. It reminded me of the channel made by an icebreaker in far northern waters.

At one place two men were busy making the channel broader. The pieces of matted vegetation which they cut off were floated out into the lake and released, in the hope that they would not float back another day when the wind blew from the opposite bank.

There were masses of water birds among the reeds and small water-hens ran about carefully on the blue hyacinth leaves; I never once saw them tread in between the leaves and get their feet wet.

The channel was over quarter of a mile long, but finally we were through and out on the open lake, where we could sail without risk of sinking a canoe.

It must have been a frightful task to paddle a canoe from one end of the lake to the other. The inhabitants did not seem, however, to regard a trip of twenty to thirty miles as anything special, but then they had a very unconventional method of propelling their craft. They stood on one leg, twisted the other around the oar and moved the boat by pushing this leg out behind—a movement which apparently required less effort than ordinary walking.

To sail with the wind is to enjoy life. These people hoist big square white sails. To me it looked dangerous with such a tall mast mounted in a narrow, flat-bottomed canoe, but they are literally born on the water and have such a fine feeling for the weather that they are always ready in advance for any squall from the surrounding mountains and can take down the sails before a catastrophe overtakes them.

We sailed past a man who was fishing for water weeds. He lowered one end of a long pole to the bottom of the lake, twisted it round a few times and, with the edge of the boat almost awash, brought up an armful of weed. He went on in this way until the boat itself was quite covered from the bow to the little platform at the stern where the fisherman stood and "walked" the boat forwards. He would then tether the water weeds in a big heap in front of his house on piles, and grow vegetables or flowers in it. Such small floating gardens may last for three to four years.

As we approached the town of Kyauktaing, all built on piles, the traffic became denser. We passed a man who was comfortably lolling alongside his umbrella, which he had attached to the bows, not to keep off the sun, but in such a way as to catch the wind which blew his boat forwards in the right direction. After a couple of hours' siesta I suppose he would be well on his way to Yawnghwe with his cargo of finely moulded earthen pots.

The honey-sweet scent of ripe pineapples told us a long way off about the cargo which the next boat was carrying. We reduced to half speed and took hold of the fruit boat. The man was delighted at the chance of business. I passed him a coin and asked him to let us have eight pineapples, but the conscientious and zealous U Maung Maung Kin protested violently, and, while the wretched fruit boat was being carried away from its destination, argued about what eight pineapples should really cost.

He took it as a gross personal insult that the price was quoted at around two shillings. The fruit-seller quickly went down to 1/6d, but U Maung Maung Kin was now angry.

At 1/4d he let it be known that he had now reached a negotiable price, although he might easily come down still lower.

"One and threepence."

U Maung Maung Kin shook his head and started to speak tolerantly to the man.

"One and tuppence," groaned the other.

At this point Kin patted him on the hand and declared in a fatherly way that he was no longer angry, but that he must ask for a reasonable price to be quoted, because he could not have his European friend so grossly cheated.

By now the fruit-seller had had enough. Once more U Maung Maung Kin put on his angry tone and said that he would try to get through the day without pineapples.

By this time they had been arguing about the price for a quarter of an hour, and our engine had carried the fruit boat so far along with us, that it would take it at least two hours to make good the loss of time, but the fruit man was reluctant to give up the chance of a deal.

"One and a penny," he said with such expression on his face that it must have been obvious, even to U Maung Maung Kin, that this was his last word.

But U Maung Maung Kin did not take his duties lightly. He began carefully to examine the individual pineapples and when we had finally secured the eight largest in the boat, U Maung paid 1/1½d and the wretched fruit-seller was at last set loose. Slowly his boat regained its original course and helped by a little sail and a yellow umbrella the scented yellow cargo floated gently away across the surface like a petal before the wind.

"Why did you pay 1/1½d, after you had spent so much time getting him down to 1/1d," I asked him in amazement.

"Oh, I have not indeed been throwing your money away. But as you know, in the large towns here in the East we always give a tip, and this fellow must be shown that we are people who are not mean about such things."

With its motor snorting our boat continued on its way towards the little country town of Inpawkon, at a speed which seemed completely out of place in such pleasant, peaceful surroundings. Small rippling waves shone like silver in the bright sunlight.

Both the cold bluish light and the situation of the lake high up among the mountains reminded me of a boat trip on Lake Titicaca two years ago. But at Titicaca the great height—about 12,000 feet—and the hard climatic conditions seemed to set an extreme limit for human existence, while here on Inle the mild weather was almost idyllic, and this one could see reflected in the people.

On Titicaca the fishermen float around on primitive artificial islands formed of rushes and reeds bound together. These were dangerous in stormy weather, and the fishermen led a daily life of privation, only managing to live on the islands for certain periods, whereas the habitations on Lake Inle are permanent.

I was also reminded, this time by the climate, of Cape Province in South Africa: Inle has an agreeable temperature, although often with a strong wind and a succession of quick showers driving across the lake. But you can see the squalls far off and so take precautions in good time, or else submit to the shower bath in good humour, because the rain is usually followed in a few minutes by brilliant sunshine.

After this long boat trip across the open waters of the lake we came

In the last rays of the sun I imagined I saw two orange-red shells in the dark pond.
They turned out to be the ears of a buffalo

Above: It's an ill wind . . . Even if the fields are flooded, the girls can always go fishing. *Below:* A market close to Lake Inle. A bunch of fine carrots costs 3d., large dahlias ½d each

to an area filled with small "islands" and "gardens" which were anchored to the bottom by long bamboo poles. A man was busy tidying up a crop of gourds. He had to sail between the rows, because the "island" would not bear his weight, but only that of the plants.

We sailed at full speed towards a 3-foot high green wall, which lay like an ice barrier in front of us.

"Are we going to sail right through it?" I asked, a little scared. We had already wasted a lot of time cleaning the propeller when it had become entangled with water plants.

"There is a lead behind it," said U Maung Maung Kin. "But sometimes they close the channels off from the lake so that water plants and grasses do not drift in and block them up."

The mechanic deftly lifted up the outboard motor, and almost unnoticeably the boat skipped over the fence, and there we were in the extensive channel system of Inpawkon.

Before we reached the town itself we came to a place where one of the broad canals was almost blocked by hundreds of canoes. We had found the floating market. I was afraid that U Maung Maung Kin would waste half a day haggling, but later on I found that his trading was an excellent way of diverting attention from my cameras. So I got a long series of colour photographs of the picturesque life in the boats.

Here there were the older women paddling in a dignified way in their clean sparkling blue everyday dresses. Like almost all Burmese they were smiling and laughing. Nevertheless they knew what they wanted, and in particular what they would pay, and had such an air of assurance that they wasted little time in bringing the traders round to their way of thinking.

It was not quite the same with the young girls in the pink *loongyis;* they were less assured in the art of buying, but on the other hand they had plenty of time. They enjoyed haggling over the price, and the traders seemed also to enjoy the whole ritual of barter with its gamut of gestures and facial expressions, enough to rouse the envy of even a great character actor.

Some of the young girls were just out for a sail; they were dressed in all their finery, with golden jewellery and flowers in their hair or else a pretty new *khamauk*, which gave them good protection against the sun.

A wrinkled old granny, busily chewing on a giant cigar, still in its band, started out at one end of the market with a canoe full of large green coconuts. She drifted slowly with the stream or pushed herself along by pulling on the edges of the neighbouring boats, until she approached the other end of the market, by which time her canoe had gradually become empty of fruit. Three coconuts were exchanged for a red comb, three for a new *khamauk*, two for a bunch of bananas, and twenty-five for a length of home-woven cloth, suitable for a *loongyi*. For ten coconuts she got some sugar, for eight some flour, and then at the coffee boat which cruised around among the traders, she got a drink of strong coffee in exchange for a single coconut. The proprietor used two saucers as castanets to announce that the coffee was freshly made.

Farther on she bartered two coconuts for a packet of tea, and gave the last ten to an old man who, with his complete workshop on board the boat, made sandals out of discarded car tyres.

The old woman was only one of the many who had made their market purchases without going to the trouble of a bank account and yet managed to afford to smoke large cigars. The potter's family brought a cargo of water-pots, the fisherman a load of fish, the weaver some lengths of material, the farmer bananas or pineapples, and so on; all was for barter.

What astonished me most was that with all these hundreds of boats, packed tight like cyclists in a Dutch town or like city commuters trying to enter the subway at rush hour, there was never a word of abuse when the boats bumped into each other.

There was one incident, however, that almost caused an upheaval. A young spark came in with his outboard motor running at full speed and caused a real commotion in the duck pond. Water overlapped into the cobbler's shop and splashed the cheroot-seller's stock. The canoes bobbed up and down against each other like paper boats in the gutter.

But only a single oar was raised to threaten the young hothead; a man picked up an egg, but he didn't throw it.

By then the young man was obviously frightened, and when his motor stalled and a false move landed him in among the rushes, the anger quickly changed to laughter and smiles.

On the way from the market into the village itself we passed a young mother who had installed her four-year-old daughter in the stern of the boat with a little child's paddle. The youngster was beaming with pride at being helmsman and did her job so conscientiously that she didn't even glance at us as we chugged past in our vulgar spluttering motor-boat.

We met a number of canoes with schoolboys—three or four in a row in each boat. They all had one leg around an oar and rhythmically "walked" the boats along. When we stopped our engine so as not to capsize their boats they began to show off. They put on speed and began to "run"; it reminded me of Norwegian boys poling themselves along on sleighs.

When the waves produced by this little race had died down and we could no longer hear the boys' rippling laughter, the silence was broken by the penetrating chimes from a *hti*, the golden top of a pagoda, where hundreds of small golden bells jingled in the wind.

I recognised the sound and a moment later I knew where I had heard it before. It is the same sound that you hear when the wind breaks up the young ice on a mountain loch and the little waves drive it in against the reeds along the shore.

With everything becoming more and more idyllic we stopped the engine which seemed increasingly out of place—like a noisy tourist in a church—and soon reached the centre of the little town.

Inpawkon is built on piles like Kampong Ayer, the water town of the Sultanate of Brunei in Borneo. But whereas Kampong Ayer is a rather depressing place—its park has only two trees and the "gardens" are merely some empty rusty petrol cans with stunted flowers—Inpawkon is green and beautiful. In front of and underneath every single house there are floating gardens with fresh green grass or rushes, flowers and pumpkins and many kinds of kitchen plants. But anyone who tried to step ashore on to such a garden would certainly step right through the thin network of roots or else carry the whole bed of floating grasses down to the bottom. All that is needed is a notice saying, "Please do not walk on the grass."

The hairdressing and barber's saloon opened out on to the water street and after treatment the customer was asked to be so good as to go down a couple of steps and rinse his own head!

The water in the canals was crystal clear. At first I wondered why the bottom sometimes seemed to change colour, as though a shadow was passing over, even though there was not a cloud in the sky at the time.

Then I observed thousands of fishes, mostly about the size of sticklebacks, swimming in big shoals beneath us.

When the children wanted to cross the street they dived head first into the water and swam across, or else they sailed over it in little coracles, which lay so low in the water that it looked as though it was only the surface tension which prevented the water from pouring in.

A canoe came towards us, filled with heavy water pots.

"What can they be for?" I asked U Maung Maung Kin. "I have seen this kind of thing in Kampong Ayer, where the houses stood in salt water, but here the water is fresh and clear."

"If we just sail on to the corner, you'll be able to see," replied U Maung Maung Kin. "The water has been brought into the town, but not yet into the houses. In some places, though, you can see a water-pipe and a tap sticking up out of the lake."

Of course he was quite right. At the next street corner a pipe emerged, for no particular reason, from the surface of the water, and a pair of twittering young girls had paddled their canoe in under the tap so that the water fell directly into their pots.

It was on this street that I heard a sound like rhythmic drill in a gymnasium.

"Do you hear the looms?" said U Maung Maung Kin. "This town is famous for producing the best *loongyis* in the whole of Burma. And there are looms in every house in this street. They are tended by young girls."

"Do men never do this work?" I asked.

"Oh, yes," he replied. "The big building at the end of the canal houses the co-operative mechanised looms, and they are worked by men only."

Just at that moment I saw a man jump head-first from a window of the building he had been talking about.

"Has he been fired?" I asked, and U Maung Maung Kin laughed. A moment later five or six other men jumped out of the windows on the first floor.

"It's just that they want to cool off; they jump out of the windows, swim round to the steps and then return to the looms again."

U Maung Maung Kin had an acquaintance in one of the houses, and when we came to the landing steps we were received by an imposing and very dignified lady. Like Kipling's Burma girl she also smoked, not however a white cheroot, but an enormous green cigar; and with blue clouds of smoke all around her she at once sent an order back over her shoulder. We heard chairs being moved about upstairs.

And then Mrs. Mi Haink, as she was called, turned towards us. U Maung Maung Kin had warned me against shaking hands—in Burma

Breakfast in the market-place. The banana-seller's eldest daughter has her face
covered with a hardened layer of powdered bark—not mud

Above: On the way to the market—with part of her body close to the water surface.
Below: The young girls in the floating market resembled brightly coloured water lilies

you do not shake women by the hand—but she herself pushed her own forward and gave me a hearty handshake, saying—in English:

"Pleased to meet you."

When we entered the house a well-laid coffee table showed that the lady had had her spies out.

She didn't know many more English words than the ones she had used when she greeted me. But she told U Maung Maung Kin that if I would do her the honour of coming again she would try to learn some more in the meantime.

Looking through the door we could see a little four-year-old boy playing out on the big balcony, which had no railing at all at the edge.

"Is that the little one's playground?" I asked anxiously.

"Yes, it is very practical. Here in a town of water he can't run wild in the forest or get away from us in any other way."

"Is it not a little risky?" I asked.

"He would be in more danger if he fell down on land or on the balcony itself, than if he fell into the water," she replied, and then gave an order through the open door.

A moment later I heard a splash and when I ran out on the balcony, saw the youngster quite cheerfully swimming around in the canal, buoyed up by a life belt of dried calabashes, which formed his only clothing from morning to evening.

Whilst we were drinking another cup of coffee we were shown some beautiful pieces of material woven from imported Chinese silk.

"Why do you not rear silkworms yourselves? The climate and the mountain slopes would be ideal for white mulberry trees."

I put the question to these industrious inhabitants of Inpawkon in the hope of getting them to give me an opinion of their compatriots in other parts of Burma, who are scarcely so energetic.

"But you know that we Buddhists may not kill; we can't destroy silkworm pupæ just for the sake of the cocoon," they replied reproachfully.

"But you have fishermen and butchers," I retorted.

"Yes, that is through necessity, and such people are not always Buddhists—at any rate not good Buddhists, and they are more or less forced into the work," said the lady, not exactly logically.

Some of the lengths of silk we were shown had strands woven of real gold thread, others silver. I was a little in doubt whether courtesy would allow me to ask the price, and if I did would they be offended if I bought nothing? Or was there a risk that they would feel obliged to present me with a length?

Instead I explained that in my country we did not use this kind of clothing material, but that it was very beautiful and as I could see very fine work.

"They cost 100 *kyats* (about 150/-) a length—but you can get one of the machine-woven *loongyis* for less than a quarter of that price," said the canny Kin.

Inside the weaving parlour the workers were mainly young girls about fourteen to fifteen years old. In all, Mrs. Mi Haink had eight weavers, but there was nothing of a factory about the workshop. The girls sat in their pretty brilliantly coloured dresses, looking like little princesses.

The sun streamed in at one window giving a glory to the black hair of a young girl who sat by it; her hair was piled up in the same way as you can see it in the old temple figures.

As we went on a group of traders came along the water street. Their trade consisted of sailing around to the houses with flour, spices, fruit and coloured sweets.

When the housewives shop they either lean dangerously out of the window or squat on the lowest step of the stairs leading up to the balcony. They are all rather plump, due no doubt to the fact that they have so little opportunity to go for a walk.

As we sailed out into Inpawkon's canals the tinkling from the golden bells on the pagoda *htis* changed its note.

"It's blowing up for a storm," said U Maung Maung Kin. "It's lucky we chose a big boat, for now all the little canoes should keep away from the open lake."

The sound of the wind, the spume and the quickly changing weather reminded me once more of wind-swept Cape Province. And now it was also becoming cold.

A little Shan boy, whom we had allowed to come with us, sat with his protruding ears beginning to freeze. He had been on a visit to some relatives in Inpawkon and was now going on to a monastery in the state of Kayah.

"Is he not too young to go into a monastery?" I asked.

"Oh, no," replied U Maung Maung Kin. "Here in Burma it is quite common for boys to spend some weeks in a monastery when they are between twelve and sixteen years old. This lad is fourteen, and a Burmese boy of fourteen is regarded as an adult and big enough to travel from one end of the country to the other."

"Ask him how he will find his way to the monastery."

"When the water lilies from Lake Inle have floated down the River Pilu for fourteen days they will come to Loi Kaw, where I am going into the monastery," replied the boy poetically. "So failing all else I can follow the river. I am sure I can easily get a job, either rowing or steering."

When I opened my mouth again to ask a question I got a piece of foam in it, so I preferred to remain silent. But the little Shan boy with the bat ears was too well started to be put off by water splashes. Soon he was soaked through, but this didn't stop him talking. From what I could hear, he was speaking about Loi Kaw. Obviously he had been there before, and when I heard the word "Padaung" I pricked up my ears. For Padaung is the race who have the so-called giraffe women, the reason for my journey.

"Tell me what he's saying," I shouted through the wind to U Maung Maung Kin.

"He is just saying that Loi Kaw is the most beautiful place in the world, with the prettiest flowers growing everywhere . . ."

"Yes, and there is a lake, which is blue, because it is completely covered with water hyacinths," said the young man suddenly in English. U Maung Maung Kin and I were both astonished.

"My father helped an English scientist who worked for four years in the forest close to where we live. I travelled around with them and we talked nothing except English. And I also played with his two children."

"What were you saying about the giraffe women?"

"Oh, yes, the giraffe women of the Padaung tribe come to Loi Kaw to visit the numerous pagodas. The finest is Taung Gwe, the Pagoda of the Split Rock."

"Yes, of course, it is the giraffe women that you are interested in," said U Maung Maung Kin. "Why don't you go to Loi Kaw?"

Now that I had seen Lake Inle I was quite prepared to sail down the River Pilu with the boy and the water hyacinths. Why not?

"But it will take you at least a fortnight to get to Loi Kaw by river," said U Maung Maung Kin, who had already got to know my tempo. He continued: "And even though my task has only been to get you to

Lake Inle, it would be a poor end to our acquaintanceship if I sent you on a tedious voyage in a flatbottomed boat—for fourteen days!"

"Last year at this time I spent three months in a canoe in the jungles of Borneo," I replied, "so I think I could stand it."

Nevertheless I must admit that fourteen days was more than I had reckoned on.

"Perhaps I can get hold of an air force plane from one of the neighbouring towns, which could put you down in Loi Kaw."

I had almost forgotten that for the moment I was a military concern, but I thanked U Maung Maung Kin, and sure enough that same evening in Taungyi he got in touch by telegraph with the air force, who promised to send a machine to a little landing strip at Heho, which was only sixty miles away.

That evening I received yet another insight into psychological warfare. I had paid U Maung Maung Kin the various expenses set out in his very meticulous accounts. I had paid a liberal, but well-earned, tip to him and his party—and was inwardly cursing a little that I should really feel the need to give him something extra because of the time and energy he had spent in saving a halfpenny here and a penny there. In the end his zeal was going to result in a deficit in the cash box.

But it was not for nothing that he belonged to a psychological department. This was apparent when, in my best oriental style and with the sealed envelope containing the tips in my hand, I had delivered a long eulogy on his many good qualities, his conscientiousness, his care for the pennies, his friendly service and so on. He asked me—with great modesty —whether he could not have two reels of my special film, of a kind that cannot be bought in Burma!

I was so taken aback that he got his films, which, of course, increased his tip by several hundred shillings. But all in all I didn't grudge it, for I am quite sure that he did not pocket one single *kyat* or *paya* of the money he administered for me on the trip.

Our vehicle was well down on its springs when we drove out to say farewell on the little landing strip. Apart from the clattering of the exhaust pipe, the whine of the distributor and a lot of other noises, which should not be heard from a well-maintained wagon, we now heard a quacking and a cackling from the back of the car, where there was a whole chicken- and duck-yard, which we had picked up for a song. Now and again there was a somewhat pained screech from a little pig which had also been bought on favourable terms. With eight big bunches of bananas, a score of cabbages and some dozens of earthenware pots, things were a bit cramped. The pig had already broken a pair of pots and had therefore taken over from me the place of honour in the driver's cabin.

It seemed they were going to have a slow journey home in the over-loaded car, but as time costs little in this country I reckoned the net profit would still be clear.

The injured voice of the pig was drowned by the revving of the aeroplane. But the aeroplane engine stopped with a bang and would not start again, and the pig continued to screech. So I decided to travel by the Pilu.

The pig was reinstalled in the rear of the car, and U Maung Maung Kin drove me back to the river.

CHAPTER IV

The River Pilu

CLOSE to where a boat-builder was busily hollowing out the hard trunk of a *thingan* tree to make a canoe I saw a large sailing canoe which lay ready to depart. Even at that distance I recognised my little friend Bat Ears.

"Welcome, sir, welcome, sir," he shouted and jumped ashore to grip me by the hand before the car had actually stopped. "Are you really coming with us?"

"Yes, indeed, if I can get a ticket to Loi Kaw," I replied.

"This boat belongs to one of my uncles. He is called Maung Chit Khaing," said Bat Ears and jumped on board to ask whether I could travel with them.

And just as U Maung Maung Kin was making a final attempt to dissuade me from such a primitive and unworthy method of transport, Bat Ears came rushing back.

"It is quite all right, sir. But we must sail now!"

I had still not taken in the fact that the term "now" in Burmese means in the course of an hour or two, so I got busy putting my baggage on board.

A little later in the day we were gliding down the River Pilu, leaving U Maung Maung Kin behind looking worried and as though, from the psychological warfare viewpoint, he was a bit offended that the aeroplane should have broken down.

Even when he had disappeared from sight I could still hear the pig, which I imagined would now be put back on to my seat in the driver's cabin. Then the engine started and the car climbed slowly, panting noisily up into the mountains.

Uncle Maung Chit was going down the river with a cargo of rice, but he also had a load of earthenware pots, which are made better and more cheaply at Lake Inle than farther south; in addition he had some coconuts and a lot of chickens in large woven baskets. The coconuts and chickens were partly intended for provisions and partly for barter on the way. The coconuts were easy to get rid of, but it was more difficult with the chickens, because so many people along the river kept chickens and ducks of their own.

In addition to the skipper, Maung Chit, and his wife and five children, there were his two young brothers with their wives and children, who came along as crew and as pleasant company. Here as everywhere in Burma pleasant company was reckoned just as important as work itself, or perhaps more important. There was a joyful mood on board, as though we were on holiday, for this was the boat's maiden voyage.

A river trip like this is undoubtedly the best way to see Burma. The engine noises are drowned by the lapping of the water against the boat, the splashing of the oars, the call of birds, the cries of children playing along the banks, and by the merry laughter of the young girls who go down to the river to bathe or wash their clothes. This laughter is so happy and pure that it sounds like an echo of the jingling golden bells in the village pagodas.

Our vessel was a little world of its own; we ate, slept and worked in intimate fellowship. The children played as they liked, apparently without anyone worrying that they might fall into the water.

We met boats that were being laboriously punted upstream; at the villages along the river we were overtaken by small fast canoes, and on a long straight stretch we hoisted sail and moved off side by side with a large boat that was loaded to the gunwales with rice. I was about to go aboard it to have a look, but Bat Ears caught hold of me, saying:

"If you do, the boat will sink."

"Oh, sorry," I replied. "I honestly thought there were special laws of nature governing boats here; I never suspected that they could sink."

"Why are they chucking those rice plants into the water," I asked, as we sailed through an extensive area of paddy-fields, where I saw some men busily throwing one bundle of rice plants after another out into the river, so that hundreds of them were floating downstream in competition with the water hyacinths.

"Conveyor belt," answered Bat Ears.

"What do you mean?"

"Just wait a bit and you will see," he replied. "I am certain you'll see somebody fishing out the plants at the first village we come to."

And sure enough, at the next bend in the river there was a little settlement and a gang of boys were busily splashing back and forth collecting up as many bunches as possible and bringing them back to land.

At the villages small boats came up alongside us to trade. Sometimes we stopped for an hour or two, and the children jumped ashore, released from their sedentary life on board.

The girls played tag or *bi-yaung-tan;* a word meaning "the comb-seller." They linked themselves together in a long chain, and the front one had to try and catch the tail of the line. I never managed to find out what the game had to do with combs.

The boys played *chinlon.* They had a light bamboo ball which they tried to keep in the air as long as possible by kicking and batting it with their hands. Five boys stood in a circle and the ball passed back and forwards between them; it seemed ages before it dropped to the ground. They were so clever at this that even the best of Europe's footballers would have looked like novices beside them. Every now and again one of them gave a solo performance. With one heel he would kick the ball up on to his head, let it roll down one arm, dance from knee to knee and from foot to foot, or grip it between his neck and shoulders, catch it between his knees, kick it with crossed legs, hurl himself out horizontally into the air, and support himself with one hand on the ground while the ball revolved between his heels. It stuck to him as though it were metal and he a magnet—as though it couldn't bear to leave him for a moment.

On board, the possibilities for play were limited, and most of the time the children were kept busy helping the adults with the work. The boys assisted by setting the sails and steering, and sometimes they also rowed; the girls helped with the cooking at the little stove.

Sometimes Maung Chit Khaing set the boys to bale out the boat. This was done with a half coconut shell, which had a stick as a handle. The children were never scolded and the atmosphere was completely happy.

The youngsters had no mechanical toys in the European sense, and were apparently not interested in dolls, or toy animals and suchlike. On the other hand they had a number of games which they played with plant seeds, such as *go-nyin.* These seeds are large and flat, about two inches across, and they come from a climbing plant in the jungle. Then there were *kha-yay-si* seeds from the tall Kha-yay tree, which early in

The little weaver, looking like a princess, will soon be superseded by Inpawkon's weaving machines, which are worked by young men

For several minutes at a time the *chinlon*-player keeps the bamboo ball dancing from foot to foot, from heel to knee and shoulder, or lets it roll down his body to be finally caught by the ankles

the season produces white scented flowers used by the women to decorate their hair, and later on produces fruits full of the seeds that the children take such a delight in. The smallest seeds were called *yvay-si;* they were seal-red with a black spot in the middle, and were a little bigger than an orange pip. Strangely enough they all weigh the same, so goldsmiths can use them as their smallest unit of weight.

With these seeds they play "heads or tails," or see who can throw nearest the jack or who can most frequently hit the other's seed. It is rather like Scandinavian children playing with marbles, but whilst in Denmark such a game often ends in disagreement and tears, I did not see a single quarrel amongst the small Burmese children. It seemed as though these little people personified not only the Oriental's love of play but also his friendly personality.

The game was broken off when mamma thought that they should pound and grind *thanaka* bark. This was done on a *kyaukpyin,* a flat round stone against which the bark was crushed and ground with a smaller stone. Sometimes the little girls sat doing this for hours at a time. The bark is mixed with water, and the paste so made is smeared on to the face in a very thick layer; there are still some who rub it all over the body. It is said to make the skin as soft as silk, and even in the towns where the best American powders are available, the women prefer to smack a good layer of bark paste on to their faces—or even just the dried bark powder.

Taken as a whole the Burmese do not fall for the products of the western world as easily as many other peoples. The women in particular are conservative. They refuse to use plastic combs, but remain faithful to their wooden combs, which are of various shapes, according to whether they are used to comb the hair or to pin it up. A good housewife will turn up her nose at aluminium cooking vessels, and anyway they would become corroded if used to prepare their harsh national food. I am astonished that the insides of the Burmese are not one big gastric ulcer, for they eat several incredibly irritating things. Fruits, for example, which are known to be poisonous, in which case they preserve their stomachs intact by taking an antidote at the same time.

They eat soup with a china spoon, and never put anything metallic into the rice, but use instead a wooden spoon, called *yaung-ma,* a word which also means sister-in-law—or anything that causes dissension. Just as the hen-pecked husband in Europe is in danger of the rolling-pin, so the Burmese man must watch out for the big wooden spoon if he has a temperamental wife. It is the facetious symbol of the feminine reign of terror.

When the work was finished Maung Chit Khaing would sit down and tell stories, especially at sunset when the supper had been dispatched, and particularly if the wind and the current could carry the boat along without help from the oars.

In spite of his relatively good command of language, little Bat Ears had the greatest difficulty in interpreting these stories for me. But he could not avoid laughing at them; often he nearly died of laughter, and if he finally succeeded in explaining them, he still never managed to make me understand what was so funny about them.

Other stories did not appeal so strongly to his sense of humour. They were moral stories of the *Struwwelpeter* type, a kind which is thought to be somewhat old fashioned nowadays; sometimes they scared both the children and women so much that they would not go ashore after dark.

In a French magazine that I had with me there was a diagram illustrating American research on rain-making. When Bat Ears saw it, he told me that he well knew how difficult it was to make rain, and that they should perhaps introduce the Burmese methods into the U.S.A. In Burma there was always plenty of rain when one had finally conjured it up.

"What do you do to make it come?"

"Well, as a rule the rain spirits, who live up in the stars, produce the rain without any fuss, but it can happen that they fall asleep, and then the sun takes over; so we awaken the rain spirits by shouting to them and drumming on empty tin-cans. It makes a frightful noise, but it helps in the end, even though they don't always wake up immediately."

It was strange to see the adult authority and dignity with which the fourteen-year-old Bat Ears behaved. He could still laugh and smile with the other children, but usually he preferred to sit and listen to the grown-ups' tales, or else he himself acted as story-teller for the little ones.

When I asked him what he had been telling them about, he nearly always explained that it was one of the Buddhist legends. Many times during the trip he had to tell of the birth of Buddha, and even though I did not understand the language I could, with the help of his intonation and by seeing the eager little faces of his audience, guess to some extent the stage he had reached in the thousand-year-old tale. The story goes like this:

Before the last of his 500-odd births Bodhisatta was living in the heaven of the contented ones, and the gods asked him to choose where on earth and by whom he wished to be born. His choice fell on Queen Maya in the town of Kapilavasthu.

One night the queen dreamed that the gods had led her to a golden mountain in the Himalayas, where Bodhisatta was wandering about in the guise of a white elephant. With great deference, the elephant walked three times round her, and then pressed itself into her right side.

At the same moment the earth shook, night became day, the blind saw, the deaf heard, the dumb spoke, the lame walked and all the musical instruments started to play on their own. There was peace, as in paradise, between the beasts and their prey, the waters of the rivers stopped flowing, the sea water turned fresh and the earth was covered with lotus flowers.

Queen Maya was making a journey when her time came, and it was in a flower garden that she gave birth to Buddha. The newborn child was welcomed by the gods and wise men, who offered him praise in gold and incense.

When the time came for him to be given a name he was called Siddhattha, his family name being Gotama, and some Brahmins prophesied that he would either become a world conqueror or a buddha. The king preferred the first alternative and did what he could to amuse the young prince by letting him live a courtly life in beautiful castles full of pretty dancing girls.

But the father could not prevent the son from seeing the bad things of life. One day on a carriage drive the prince met an old man who was shivering, another day one who was sick, and shortly afterwards he saw a funeral procession. These experiences made such an impression on the future Buddha that he no longer enjoyed the performances of the dancing girls when he returned to his castle.

When Prince Siddhattha eventually fell asleep, the beautiful girls also lay down to sleep, but a little later the prince woke up, and when he saw how the women lay snoring or with open mouths or in ugly positions he was filled with disgust. To him they looked like corpses and he decided to ride away immediately.

As he left the castle, the gate sprang open by itself and the gods held their hands underneath the horse's hooves. Flowers rained down from heaven over the chosen one in such quantities that his horse was trotting through flowers up to its belly, and that is why in that one night the future Buddha "only" managed to ride through three kingdoms.

During this part of the story I could follow the increasing interest in the faces of the little children, but this was very quickly lost when the story continued with Buddha's fight to save the world by an asceticism that in the end brought him to live on a single grain of rice a day.

He just managed not to starve completely, and after he had come to the conclusion that extreme abstinence was not the right way he met the prince of evil, the tempter Mara, who sought to frighten Buddha with his power. Buddha defeated a large army, which was seventy miles long and led by Mara himself, riding on an elephant which reached right up to heaven.

Now the children were again interested and they shouted with joy when Bat Ears told them about Buddha's victory.

After that came Buddha's enlightenment and his first sermon, the Benares sermon, which corresponds to Jesus's Sermon on the Mount.

The little fourteen-year-old teacher sat Buddha-like with crossed legs and now turned to face me (for this was the most "adult" part of the story); he spoke as though he were my teacher and of equal age or older. He was so serious and rehearsed his beliefs in such detail that I was completely captivated.

The Benares sermon is the essence of Buddhist thought. After a week of meditation in the forest near Benares, where he sat under the sacred *bo* tree, Buddha received his enlightenment, and at the same moment that the secret life was revealed to him, red blossoms rained down from the tree, although this was not the flowering season.

Buddha saw existence as a chain, as a circle of evil, but he also realised that he could break it at its weakest point—desire. This was the concept which allowed him to point the way to Nirvana, the concept which made him Buddha. When dawn broke, more miracles occurred, just as at Buddha's conception.

And now with the enumeration of the many wonderful occurrences —trees covered with fruits, the sick cured and so on—the young ones began to embroider on the story themselves; they became so wrapped up in it that I was sure that more and more miracles were invented each time the story was told. They completely took over the recital from Bat Ears, who with true Buddhist resignation smilingly submitted.

When the children had talked a bit too much nonsense, and had mentioned every tree which produces wonderful flowers and fruit, Bat Ears came over to me. In order to test his knowledge I said:

"Can you tell me what it was that was revealed to Buddha that day in the forest at Benares?"

Bat Ears had the Benares sermon at his fingertips:

"There are two extremes, O ye monks, which he who has renounced the world must not become addicted to. What are these two? One consists of indulging in sensual pleasures; this is vulgar, coarse, banal, profane and futile. The other consists of asceticism; this is painful, profane and unprofitable. Without indulging in either of these two extremes the perfect man, O ye monks, has found a middle path which opens his eyes, awakens his understanding and leads to peace, to insight, to the higher wisdom and to Nirvana, And what, O ye monks, is this middle path, which the perfect man has found, and which opens his eyes, awakens his understanding and leads to peace, to insight, to the higher wisdom and to Nirvana? It is the noble eight-fold path: that is to say, right views, right aspirations, right speech, right conduct, right habits, right effort, right mind control, and right meditation. This is the middle path, O ye monks, which the perfect man has found, and which opens his eyes, awakens his understanding and leads to peace, to insight, to the higher wisdom and to Nirvana. Such, O ye monks, is the noble truth about suffering: birth is attended with pain, sickness is painful, death is painful, to be separated from something loved is painful, and any unsatisfied craving, that too is painful; in brief, the five ties that bind us to existence are painful. Such, O ye monks, is the noble truth about the origin of suffering: it is the craving which causes the renewal of our being, that is accompanied by sensual delights and seeks satisfaction, now here, now there; it is the craving for pleasure, the craving for a future life, and for power. Such, O ye monks, is the noble truth about the passing away of suffering; it consists in completely ending this craving, in giving it up, in putting it away from oneself, in freeing oneself from it, in harbouring it no longer. Such, O ye monks, is the noble truth about the path that leads to the passing away of suffering: it is the noble eight-fold path: right views, right aspirations, right speech, right conduct, right habits, right effort, right mind control and right meditation.

"It is very easy to understand," continued Bat Ears. "Buddha suddenly discovered how everything hung together: death comes from old age, old age from birth, birth from desire and desire from the senses, which we are born with. Their power depends on the deeds we have committed in an earlier life, and the heritage is heavy to bear if we are ignorant, and ignorance is therefore the reason for all misery. But Buddha has given us his doctrine; he has shown us that there *is* something we can do and that is to fight desire. By fighting all sorts of desire, for money and power and so on, we will become liberated and able to save ourselves."

"And can one also improve oneself through one's karma?" I asked, and Bat Ears continued learnedly:

"Karma is the sum of all the things that you have done in your life. If you draw up an account of all your good and less good deeds you will get a result which depends entirely on you yourself—and you will make your own happiness; it is not the same as in other religions where prayers and divine intervention and so on may also be important. We Buddhists do not believe in these," he said emphatically.

"So karma is in our soul and lives on when we are reborn, and is there until eternity?" I asked, trying to draw him.

But little Bat Ears would not let himself be caught. He raised his hand in warning, looked at me seriously and said:

"Buddha says that we must not discuss the soul and eternity. There are two extremes we must avoid," he continued. "One extreme is to pursue the satisfaction of the passions and sensual enjoyment; Buddha says that this is degrading and low. The other extreme is self-torture and excessive asceticism—this is painful and useless."

"Tell me then about the right road, the middle path," I said.

"It is the eight-fold path, where we think right, where we show the right and complete will, complete speech, complete actions, complete occupation."

"You must also not be a hunter or a fisherman?" I interjected.

"No!" said Bat Ears. "For then you don't respect life. And you must show complete pursuit of the right, complete vigilance and reflection and complete absorption."

"By complete absorption do you mean mind control?" I asked.

"Yes," he replied and tried to explain the concept more accurately, but either mindfulness is too abstract a concept for me or else Bat Ears in spite of his excellent English was at a loss, for he came to a halt. But as a good teacher should, little Bat Ears summed up the crux of the Benares sermon by saying that Buddha teaches that one can abolish suffering by fighting the egoistical desire for existence and its enjoyment.

"But the Christians' Jesus also said, 'lay not up for yourselves treasures upon earth'," I remarked.

"But surely that's just what you do in the western world, is it not?" he replied.

There was an uneasy pause and then I tried again to lure Bat Ears into talking about Nirvana, but here he called a halt. My learned friend explained quite patiently that Nirvana lay outside the comprehension of man, and so it would be wrong to waste time in discussing it.

Then with his index finger raised, his voice solemn and such a serious expression on his face that I only just managed to avoid laughing, he finished his tutorial by telling me about the scribes and the elephant.

"When learned men dispute, Buddha compares them to a group of blind men who are put in front of an elephant and asked to say what it is. One man feels the elephant's belly and says it is a barrel. Another feels a front leg and says it is the bole of a tree. A third feels the trunk and says it is a water-snake, and a fourth who has got hold of the tail says it is a broom. And he who has seized an ear declares that it is a fan. Each one of them has only got hold of a tiny part of the truth and therefore they cannot agree."

Occasionally we spent the night ashore with acquaintances of Maung Chit Khaing, and one evening we were even invited to dinner with one of his friends who was a prosperous merchant.

I had hoped that we should eat in the Burmese style, but in my honour the low table was moved aside and replaced by European tables. What astonished me most was the young girl who crawled under the table, sat down and began to wave a fan.

"Do the Burmese have warmer feet than other people?" I cautiously asked my omniscient Bat Ears.

"No, the girl is fanning away the mosquitoes, so that they don't bite our bare ankles."

Most Burmese try to keep off beer and spirits, but as they had a European guest they served wine, and fortunately they had no small wine glasses, but only large tumblers. The wine was excellent and its effect splendid.

The good Maung Chit Khaing got up and began to speak in a language which even I knew was not Burmese. I guessed that it must be the sacred tongue of Buddhism, but a little later I realised that he had been speaking in English, and in my honour. So I had to stand up and deliver a short address of thanks, using the few words of Burmese that I had learned and these the other side didn't understand either!

This was the only time I have been in Buddhist company where the tone was what in Europe we would call merry. However, nobody ended up under the table, in spite of the pretty girl who sat there patiently fanning our ankles.

One evening, when we had a long straight stretch of river ahead of us, and a favourable wind and current, we decided to sail on through the moonlight. The women wrapped themselves up in rugs and plaited mats and lay down to sleep amidships, whilst we men sat up in the bows.

There was obviously something weighing on Bat Ears' mind, and after some reflection he came out with it. He was distressed, he said, that he had drunk alcohol while on his way to the monastery, for this is against the tenets of Buddhism, and Bat Ears dearly wanted to be a good man.

Then he began to speak of a Buddhist hell with innumerable departments where sinners must suffer for their misdeeds. There were punishments which could easily be related to those imagined by Christians through the ages.

In addition to fire and burning coals, Bat Ears' hell also had boiling oil, hot knives and unpleasant mythical creatures—dogs with gruesome mouths and giant vultures that tore the flesh from the bones of the guilty. I had a very bad conscience because it was my fault that they had served wine to the zealous little Buddhist.

"I thought that there was no hell in the Buddhist faith. You didn't speak about it the other day."

"No, there isn't one really," replied Bat Ears, a little shyly. "But nevertheless many people can't avoid thinking about it, and by the way, the Englishman I once knew said that some of you also believe in it."

All at once his gloomy expression disappeared and he spoke once more about the good Buddha, who shows the way to Nirvana by his example. When Bat Ears had been speaking about "the 80,000 large hells and the 40,040 small hells," and the tortures laid on in them, his face had been full of portent, but now he was again filled with joy.

He talked about Mount Myinmo, the largest mountain in the world, which is a million miles high, and goes down for a million miles into the sea. It is on this mountain that Buddhism's *dewas*, the divine spirits, live, and also the righteous *byammas* who are placed up on the slopes in

Above left: An elephant woman, with several pounds of steel wire round her knees, pounding millet. *Above right:* A five year old boy from the "floating village" at Lake Inle, with a life-belt of calabashes. *Below left:* "No man can rule over women. They just do what they themselves want" said the old Padaung chief. *Below right:* It is alleged that the long necks are a result of excessive vanity

The giraffe women maintain that they wear the neck spiral as a protection against
tiger bites

Left: The Padaung woman cannot see her child when suckling it. *Above right:* Giraffe women, bending over to see the earth they are cultivating, look rather like real giraffes. *Below right:* It is regarded as a great compliment to put out your tongue

Above left: The abbot with his pet rabbit. *Above right:* The children's procession on its way to Taung Gwe, the Pagoda of the Split Rock. *Below:* These giraffe women have lit wax candles in front of Buddha

a hierarchy determined by the perfection of their nature. On top of all is Nirvana, the Buddhists' paradise.

Bat Ears also talked about some islands with lovely trees, that lie near to this mountain; one of them is reserved for Buddhists who here improve themselves for a further thousand years, before they reach Nirvana. Another island is kept for the English (and here Bat Ears surely meant all non-Buddhists) but there the conditions were scarcely so good as on the Buddhists' island.

"Deep down in the sea," he mentioned in passing, "are the hells—more than 40,000 of them—that is *if* they exist."

I was afraid that my little teacher was being rather fanciful. It was difficult for me to follow him and in particular difficult to find a connection between all this and the rational account he had given me the other day.

"I really can't see that what you're telling me now has anything to do with Buddhism," I said bluntly.

"No, it hasn't," he admitted. "Most of it is just old folk tales, which have nothing at all to do with Buddhism. That is why I am going into a monastery again to hear the true learning. I have become too superstitious."

"So you've been in a monastery before?"

"Yes, when I was nine years old. For in Burma most men go into a monastery several times during their life. Sometimes only for a week or two, if for example they've been in a war or have behaved wrongly in some other way, or if they think, as in my case, that they have forgotten the true teaching of Buddha. Then they will re-enter the monastery for a time."

"Why was the skipper so angry this afternoon when I wanted to break a branch off that big tree near the river? Had it anything to do with true Buddhism—or was it superstition?"

"A *nat* or spirit lives in the tree, and it would become angry if you damaged the tree."

"What has that got to do with Buddha?" I asked once more.

"Not much, really, in fact nothing, but nevertheless we believe that the *nat*-spirits can help us in need. Buddha only shows us the way to behave correctly, but it is rather different with a *nat*-spirit. It is easier to come to an arrangement with one of them, and you can often see bowls and pots with flowers or rice placed under the *nat*-trees as offerings. But naturally we don't learn anything about *nat*-spirits in the monastery."

At this point I gave up trying to understand more about Buddhism and wrapped myself up in a blanket to get some sleep.

At dawn the next morning, just as we were sailing under the bridge at the town of Samka, I heard someone shouting and then the familiar sound of an engine, which backfired every now and again. Shortly afterwards, when I heard the screech from a displeased pig, I knew that I really was awake.

It was of course U Maung Maung Kin, who had driven over with the whole of his crew, plus the bananas, cabbages, earthenware pots, chickens and pig, to tell me that the aeroplane was now working and that he would take me back to the landing strip so that I could travel to Loi Kaw in the only way proper for a European. He had driven the whole night to overtake us here in Samka, for farther down the river the motor road had been broken up by the rains.

Fortunately I had now seen something of life on the river, and even though I would have preferred to continue in the same way, I just could not say no to the loyal U Maung Maung Kin. So I bade farewell to the little world of the boat.

The pig was again moved to the back of the car and I took up the place of honour in the driver's cabin. Once more we set off for the landing strip at Heho, which we should reach in about twenty-four hours.

Au revoir in Loi Kaw, Bat Ears!

CHAPTER V

Loi Kaw

THE AIRCRAFT was now flying at full speed; I was approaching my goal. Thanks to the river trip I had now formed my own impression of the Burmese. I had learned to value their friendliness towards strangers and knew that I was sure of a roof over my head, if only I could find some of the people whose names I had obtained through friends of friends.

Loi Kaw, which lay in a bay off the River Pilu, was a pleasant little country town, with nothing but wooden houses. The brown water of the river flowed past in a broad sweep, carrying with it thousands upon thousands of bobbing water hyacinths, from Lake Inle to the big Salween River, which they reach after a journey of some three weeks. From the water's edge you could hear the merry laughter of the Burmese girls. Mothers with two or three children were so slim and well-built that they looked like fourteen-year-old girls.

Loi Kaw had only one main street. Here the Orient's ubiquitous Indians had their stalls and shops. In addition there was a Malayan photographer and a Chinese dentist, who had painted over his door a giant set of false teeth, which looked as though they were intended to scare away his clients. When open for business the wall facing the street was removed and there right in the middle of his shop, in full view of the public, stood an enormous and awe-inspiring dentist's chair, looking like the electric chair in Sing Sing. Perhaps in its own way the latter is more merciful.

A motley crowd of spectators quickly gathered in front of the shop whenever a victim sat down in the chair. To the ordinary people of Loi Kaw this clinic provided excellent entertainment—after all the town had so few amusements. The tender little Burmese girls shuddered when the patient screamed, but it was very seldom that the victim made any sound, even if the primitive foot-operated drill did make him feel as though he was being treated by a road-mender.

A tooth extraction was going on just as I passed by. It was obvious that this was the rôle which the dentist most enjoyed. Like an ambitious amateur actor his preparations were careful and exaggerated; he turned his sleeves up far above the elbows and as the performance reached its climax stretched out for the big pair of forceps. With a triumphal gesture he held up a bloody molar and finally cast it out on to the road, where a dog carefully sniffed it, before being driven off by a couple of boys who collected molar teeth.

It was characteristic that the spectators outside the establishment were never mischievous, but only interested. In all aspects of life this race seems to be marked by smiles, friendliness and tolerance. The tooth extraction was undoubtedly good publicity, and certainly much better than the giant set of jaws painted over the shop, which looked as though it had been constructed for a whale.

A couple of so-called elephant women stopped and gazed sceptically at all this modern technique. They belonged to the Kayah tribes, who live in villages in an undulating forest terrain hundreds of miles from Loi Kaw, where they exist by growing maize and root vegetables and keeping pigs.

These women have been so named because they walk around with ten to twelve pounds of steel wire coiled around each knee. You might think that this was very inconvenient, but the women carry their burden with a smile and are always happy and cheerful. Even though the steel coils caused them to walk with straddled legs they were by no means unattractive. But they are very shy, so it is only rarely that a couple will allow themselves to be lured into Loi Kaw to buy glass beads or steel wire from the Indians; doubtless they themselves would die of shame if they had to sit exposed in the dentist's chair.

Sometimes also a medicine man came in from the wilds, and with scarcely concealed envy would watch the success of his colleague, the Chinese dentist.

When I arrived in Loi Kaw I had four or five addresses in my pocket— the addresses of acquaintances of people whom I had met by chance. A couple of Burmese were standing by an old lorry and they seemed to be in no hurry, so I showed them my list; this was written in European and Burmese script, so it should not have raised any big problems. But evidently the two men found it difficult to decipher, either because of poor eyesight, or because it was badly written, or more likely because they were not much good at the art of reading. But with a joint effort we solved the riddle and chugged off to the first address.

We stopped outside a distinguished looking-house, and a man-servant, who knew very little English, explained to me with some difficulty that the family was away on a trip, but that I could come in with my baggage. However this seemed to me to be a bit too brash, and even though all my baggage had been carried into the house, I finally put a big cross against it and told my assistants that I wanted to drive on to the second address.

This turned out to be a fine teak house. A big servant-girl, who had been sweetly slumbering in a rocking-chair on the veranda, suddenly became so active that she promptly tried to drag me inside. She pulled energetically on one side of my aluminium box; evidently she mis-understood my resistance and was so zealous that she nearly pulled both me and the box inside at the same time. But here too there was nobody at home, so with the help of another big cross against the second address I avoided being committed to the muscular lady, and the lorry plodded on through the mud.

At the third address the house was closed and locked up, but one of my two assistants coolly clambered in at a window, shot the bolt from the inside and said I should just make myself at home. Another big cross. I don't like to be too fussy, but there are limits to my audacity.

For a moment my friends seemed to be a little irresolute while they discussed the actual location of the fourth address, but we drove off and about six miles outside the town stopped in front of a miserable little house. When we entered some youngsters fled screaming with terror, and a young girl dashed out across the flooded paddy-field to seek consolation with a team of water buffaloes. Shortly afterwards came a little thin man who was pale grey from head to toe from the splashing of the water buffaloes. He stared at us, at first apprehensively, as though we had come to take his poor property from him. Eventually we found out that this was the wrong address, and so we drove back to the town, much to the relief of the little grey man.

It is always difficult to decipher Burmese writing, but a man whom we stopped on the street apparently put us on the right track for soon afterwards we were driving off in a new direction. Then we ran into a lashing rainstorm. My two guides insisted that I should sit between them in the driver's cabin, for the car doors had long since disappeared and the rain was pouring in on us.

I was a little embarrassed at receiving so many kindnesses from complete strangers, but it was no use my protesting; I just had to sit in the middle and watch my two benefactors becoming soaked through. I also got my own little share of the wet, for it was soon apparent that the roof leaked, and—what was worse—the muddy red water from the soft road splashed up through the wagon, because there were gaps between the floorboards in the driver's cabin. At any rate, I thought, they will get a tip which will go towards a new floor.

Suddenly the lorry stopped; they had thought of something. One of them jumped up on to the back of the lorry in the streaming rain so that I could have my really very watertight tropical boxes in alongside me. Now I really was sorry that I could not speak Burmese. But the two men only laughed and the first one just beamed with joy at being allowed to get extra soaked for the sake of the boxes. This was becoming too expensive, I thought, but it would have been wrong to protest, since they obviously wanted to do it. Besides it's rather difficult to protest when you don't know the language.

The fourth address looked like a hen-house. A man came out in the rain and the address list was consulted. Yes, this was the right place.

The rain stopped as quickly as it started and I took a closer look at the hen-house. My first impression was quite correct; it had originally been built as a rest-house and inside there were still some rickety old beds. But apparently they had had more use for a hen-house—in any case there were hens everywhere. But I have never been much in favour of going early to bed with the hens.

Again a big cross, and we set off for the fifth and last address. If this one failed I began to think that there was nothing for it but to drive back and try to get a bed—or a perch—in the hen-house.

Address No. 5. Eureka! Mr. Reza, plantation owner, cinema director and businessman was at home. And he was not at all worried that I could not find out from my notes from which friend of a friend I had obtained his address.

"I wonder whether you could tell me where I could stay for a few days?" I asked cautiously.

"You can stay here. My guest room is empty and I am a bachelor. Actually I would like to have some company," replied Mr. Reza. I modestly declined his invitation a suitable number of times—and then settled in.

While the baggage was being carried up to the guest room my

two wet friends tried to decamp. I rushed in and fetched Reza who was at a meeting in his office.

"I haven't paid for the lorry; how much do I owe? Please ask them!"

When Reza had translated my question the two men grinned and shook their heads.

"Not a penny."

"Yes, but I must pay. I can't receive help for half a day without paying for it."

"These two chaps like to help people. They'll only be offended if you offer them money."

"Then I must give them a present. Will you ask for their address so that I can send them something?"

But, laughing all over their faces, the two helpful men stepped on the gas, waved good-bye and the lorry disappeared with mud splashing around the wheels, and leaving behind a blue haze of exhaust gases. I had received a new lesson in the helpfulness of the Burmese.

At supper I was talking about the smiling friendliness I had met everywhere in Burma.

"What are people like in other countries?" asked Reza.

"It is difficult to generalise, but when I have asked the way in New York the man I have asked has often rushed away, almost offended that I should delay his *way of living!* In Africa, on the other hand, I have always been able to get an answer, but have several times been put on the wrong road, because a negro would rather give wrong information than acknowledge his ignorance. In Hong Kong I have been driven half-way round the town so that the taxi-meter should clock up the greatest possible figure, and in Cairo I have been asked an exorbitant price for assistance—that is before Nasser came to power; nowadays things are much changed."

"And in your own country?" asked Reza.

"Oh, yes, in Denmark it is an article of faith that we are the best and the nicest and most helpful people in the whole world, but I am afraid that we could nevertheless learn an awful lot from the Burmese."

When we had reached the coffee stage the conversation turned to Buddhism and the other great religions, and I waded right in.

"As the saying goes everybody is happy in his own beliefs—in basic principles most religions are just about as good as the next one," I said and carelessly continued. "But personally I can't really appreciate the Moslems. They are too fanatical, and . . ."

I stopped at once when I saw Reza's face suddenly stiffen.

There was a long pause.

"I am a Moslem," he said.

Another pause.

"I am afraid that I have expressed myself too categorically to be able to repair the damage without becoming even more involved."

"My father would be offended, but I am not a fanatic," said Reza. "I have many friends amongst the Buddhists in this town, but my ancestors believed in Allah, and so I also became a Moslem. What is that you have against Islam?"

"I have recently been in Saudi Arabia," I replied. "And I can't bear the mentality you meet there, which is apparently derived from Islamic teaching. Their intolerance and hatred of other beliefs is diametrically opposed to everything that I admire in Buddhism, with its humanity and its understanding of the viewpoint of others."

"I can well understand what you mean," answered Reza. "And that is one of the reasons why I am not a particularly fanatical Moslem."

This little interlude did not impair our friendship (for Reza *was* by no means a fanatical Moslem), and soon we were busy making plans.

Reza's hospitality and readiness to help were in no way inferior to those shown by my two friends with the lorry. Apparently he had nothing else to do but to help me, and I soon learnt that I could stay with him as long as I liked. He was almost offended when I offered to pay for my keep. But Reza was very interested in photography, and when I saw him admiring my lightweight electronic flash with its modern transistor system I knew what I should give him in return for his help.

In the hope of reaching the village of my giraffe women in about a week's time, at the latest, I said that I would like to drive around for a couple of days—but here there was absolutely no trace of the *mañana* mentality I had met in other tropical countries, for within two days we were ready to start.

So as not to waste the forenoon Reza drove me out to see his coffee plantation. Reza had Indian blood in his veins, and it must have been this that made him more interested in business than the Burmese usually are. He was one of those people who, when they get a new idea, go in for it body and soul. And at this moment Reza's hobby was coffee.

As we scrambled over fences, and waded through swamps to reach the area he had bought, he outlined for me the great potentialities behind coffee-growing.

Burma is a splendid country for coffee, but the lack of initiative in the population means that they still have to import it. So the Government is now distributing free coffee plants, on condition that the recipient prepares the holes for planting—which is in fact quite a big job. When we reached the coffee field I saw that hundreds of bushes had already been planted, and in another part of the area a couple of Burmese were busy digging. The hole has to be a cubic yard in volume, and a labourer gets about a shilling for digging one. The land here has only cost a few pounds per acre and at the end of four to five years each coffee bush should yield some forty pounds of coffee annually. Reza, who was enthusiastic about his plantation, waved his arms and said:

"At the moment I am planting 5000 bushes and I plan to put in a further 5000 every year. If you multiply the forty pounds by the number of bushes I have planted and then multiply the result by the price of coffee per pound it adds up to quite a tidy sum of money."

I asked Reza whether he knew the Danish author Hans Christian Andersen—and in particular the story of "The Women and the Eggs."

"Yes," he replied. "That poem is rather well known here in Burma, and I must admit that you are not the first to mention it when I have been talking about my coffee. But even if the price drops by half, and even if the bushes only give half the average yield, and even if half the plants die——"

Reza was again absorbed in his calculations on coffee yields, when I noticed that some of the bushes looked a little limp.

"Yes," said Reza. "In the last four days we have planted 1,500 bushes, and if there is no rain during the next day or two these new plants will all die. But even if only an eighth of my coffee plants grow . . ."

CHAPTER VI

Theatre

WHILST my little expedition to the giraffe women was in preparation I saw a remarkable theatre performance.

The owner of the local gaming saloon had recently been a little too successful—or a little too cunning; at any rate the Burmese, who love gambling, had become somewhat dissatisfied with him. In any other country the affair would probably have caused a scandal and might have ended in a law suit. But here in Loi Kaw the problem was solved in a splendid way: by getting the owner of the casino to put on a free theatre performance, which anyone who wanted could attend. Good relations with his customers would thereby be restored.

"We must eat a little earlier this evening," said my host, "because the whole of my staff want to go to the theatre afterwards."

"It is gratifying that they have such good taste," I replied and pictured to myself the Theatre Royal in Loi Kaw style. "You told me that most of them spend their time gambling."

"I don't think you quite understand the position," laughed Reza. "So I'll explain about the casino owner and his free theatre performance."

"I would rather like to see it."

"That's easy to do and it won't cost you a penny. But perhaps your feet will get a bit wet, because it's taking place on the outskirts of the town, and there has been a lot of rain."

When we had finished our meal we drove off through the little town, over the wooden bridge and farther on in the direction of Taung Gwe monastery. Just before the monastery Reza backed into a side road, and began to reverse up it.

"Why are you driving backwards?" I asked in astonishment.

"Well, it's just to protect ourselves really. I want to back as far as possible until we get stuck in the mud; then we'll leave the car and walk the last bit. We can always find someone to pull the car out when we want to go home and so it is important that it should face the right way." And suddenly we were stuck fast.

I thought we must either have lost the back wheels or else have fallen into a ditch. But evidently we had only landed in a hole in the road, which was just a touch bigger than the others.

"We can safely leave the car here," said Reza. "Nobody is likely to borrow it. It would be too difficult."

When we stepped out I immediately got the wet feet Reza had promised me. It was pitch dark, but if we could not see where we were going we could at least hear where the festivities were going on, for the darkness was pierced by raucous music from a loudspeaker system.

We turned the corner at a wooden stall and the din struck us full force. There was no sign of a theatre building, only something that looked like a colossal hay-barn: an enormous corrugated iron roof supported on twenty to thirty stout posts. This was the theatre!

There was a primitive stage which had obviously been rigged up for the occasion. The orchestra pit was just a hole in the ground, but the musicians had moved off elsewhere, because it had been flooded by the rain. The hall of the theatre had no walls, but this did not matter, for there was no admission charge, as the performance was being paid out of the big profit made by the local casino owner on bingo and other games of chance. There were none of the traditional divisions of a theatre, with arm-chairs in front and wooden benches at the back, for there were in fact no chairs at all. You just sat yourself down on the ground.

The audience started to arrive around seven o'clock and for about two hours they were entertained by the ear-splitting noise from the loudspeaker. It sounded inconceivably dreadful, but out in the East they are inclined to judge mechanically produced music by its strength. And yet the theatre orchestra, which began to play at about nine o'clock, produced some rather good music, which even a European ear could appreciate.

As the performance was to last until dawn it is not surprising that there were three complete orchestras, in addition to the frightful gramophone records. At first each orchestra played in turn, but as the night wore on things got in a muddle, for either professional loyalty—or perhaps some sort of gentleman's agreement—demanded that when a musician fell asleep he should be left in peace until he woke up and that in the meantime his place should be taken by a man from one of the other orchestras. In addition to the stool on which he sat when playing, each musician had a deck-chair, and as far as I could make out the only thing the playing musicians could do to get relieved was to increase the din. This was quite easy for the big drums, but more difficult for the pianist, even though he hammered away so hard that pieces of the ivory keyboard flew off from time to time.

Up on the stage there were several teams in action. Reza could not decide whether there were two or three troupes of actors taking part. He guessed there were two, but drew my attention to the fact that there were a number of free-lance actors, the local talent, who now and then took over a part, much to the amusement of their fellow-townsmen.

Nor could Reza give me a clear picture of the plot—or plots—that were being enacted on the stage. But when two of the leading actors sprang up on to the stage and after a little scuffle flung another actor over the edge, Reza could swear to it that the ejected man was a free-lance, and that his appearance was not part of the programme.

The actors seemed to throw themselves into their parts; they shouted, screamed and gesticulated so wildly with their arms and legs, that if anything they reminded me of puppets in the hands of an over-excited child.

It seemed as though competition were essential to this drama-marathon. Whenever the sound of the tropical rain beating against the tin roof made it impossible for the audience to hear even the loudest scream from the stage, the whole thing degenerated into a sort of pantomime and the gesticulations became even wilder than before.

The rain had the upper hand for about an hour, but it ceased quite suddenly, and then the actors seemed to be recharged with histrionic vigour. On several occasions both troupes of actors were on the stage at the same time, each group acting its own play. So the audience had a free choice, and could follow the performance which appeared the best—or at least they could try to follow it.

This was truly a family occasion. There were even babies in the theatre, who quickly fell asleep in spite of the din. The women with children kept at a suitable distance from the noisy stage; they preferred the middle places, where they could follow the performances and also had the chance of a little nap; and of course there was no danger of anyone

An oriental theatre is something quite unique. In the upper picture the man is acting the part of a local Jean de France, who had acquired affected mannerisms in England. *Below:* Quite apart from the scheduled programme, and with the curtain up, the "Wood-sprite" tries to flirt with the little theatre's prima ballerina

The school-room has no teacher's desk and no tables for the pupils. The teacher
sits on a step and the children lie on the floor, their tongues following the pencils as
they wander over the slates

falling off a chair while sleeping. They woke up now and again in the course of the night—if the children cried or if there was some particularly deafening noise from the stage.

Those men who did not sit with their families seemed to prefer the seats at the back or on the outside, where they had peace for a game of cards and the chance to go out and stretch their legs.

One little family who appeared to have come a long distance had brought a goat kid with them. It didn't get any special treatment but played with the boys and girls of the family and slept with them—but it didn't show any interest at all in what was going on on the stage.

Later in the evening it became hungry and gave out heart-rending cries, and shortly afterwards I saw an exasperated "inspector" making his way in towards the little family. I asked Reza to follow and find out whether they were going to be chucked out into the darkness. But to my relief they were allowed to remain sitting where they were, complete with children and goat.

Reza told me that the father of the family had explained that they had come a long distance and that as nobody had yet wanted to buy the kid they had by necessity to have it with them the whole time—even in the theatre.

Peanuts and baked bean rissoles were served on the road outside which acted as a foyer. There were smoking carbide lamps instead of chandeliers and five inches of mud instead of a carpet; nevertheless the place had atmosphere. A lot of fizzy lemonade—coloured river water—was drunk and so many of the big green Burma cheroots were smoked that the "theatre hall" was quite foggy in spite of the lack of walls. One thing is certain: nobody in the theatre was bitten by mosquitoes that night!

During the rain showers space became rather cramped, because a score of cycles had been brought in under the theatre roof. But soon there was elbow room again and it was possible to stretch your legs, and this meant that over half of the audience was sound asleep before midnight; and the loud snoring acted as a stimulus to increase the tempo on the stage. In the middle of one song we saw the theatre management come forward and forcibly drag the actors out into the wings. Then—probably only to awaken their public—they played a short piece about a bandit attack, in which the war drums and the blunderbusses recalled the slumberers to the unreal reality of the theatre. The big orchestra drums, assisted by two wash-tubs, gave a flourish, which sounded like a clap of thunder.

One of the boys climbed on to the piano and relieved himself. This caused a bit of fuss, but the instrument's tone became no less false on this account.

The grotesque performance now shifted scene faster and faster; back-cloths and curtains were raised and lowered incessantly. On two occasions the curtain came down on the heads of the actors, much to the amusement of the audience.

In the middle of all this a dancing girl came in apropos of nothing, whilst a man was changing costume from hero to villain. She danced as though she had just trodden in something sticky and finally fell down on the floor with a crash.

"The final scene of *Swan Lake*," whispered Reza.

The theatre director came down to see me. He was honoured to be visited by a European. I had only to shout loudly if there were any scenes I would like repeated so as to get photographs. And by the way, would I be so kind as to come up on the stage and take part in a couple of scenes? I could either be the hero who chases the wild jungle man off the stage, or I could be the judge who only has to sit and nod. It was indeed a tempting offer, but much to his disappointment I declined. This he just could not understand: to be allowed to play a lover on a Burmese stage and to save the beautiful . . .

"Which is the beauty?" I asked.

"Over there, the one with the two upper front teeth missing," he said.

Among the audience there were some Gurkha women with rings in their noses. They had come from the northern Shan states, and it was obvious that they thought the performance so exceptional that they were not going to miss anything by falling asleep. Later in the evening Reza came to life. He had suddenly found out about one of the plots. The piece was about a young man, he explained, who had been in England for a year and had become completely spoilt. He had acquired English mannerisms, walked stiffly like a soldier, shook hands with women— which in Burma is almost regarded as improper—and used English words which meant something rude in Burmese. In short, he behaved rather like Holberg's Jean de France. And when he proposed to a pretty young Burmese girl the laughter became so loud that most of the sleepers awoke.

But there was absolutely nothing malicious in this satire—people have long ago forgiven the British for having once occupied the country—it was just good clean fun.

The performers were painted with a make-up which looked as though it had been smacked on with a tar brush or a trowel, and to a European the colour combinations were horrible—probably because the dresses were a mixture of Burmese cloth in Burmese colours and European cloth in European colours. The prima donna had letter-box-red lips, blue eyebrows, a reddish-yellow wig and cheeks like an alcoholic. Her blouse was lilac-red, and she wore a skirt which in both colour and shape reminded me of an Edam cheese. She had golden sandals on her feet, but they must have been pinching, for in the middle of the twentieth act she placed them out in the wings.

The back-cloth showed a castle in a rather unusual perspective, and the flies depicted a jungle, with snakes, suspended monkeys and an awe-inspiring tiger's head; both *Swan Lake* and the bandit attack were shown against this romantic setting. The curtain was mainly used to get the energetic actors off the stage, when shouting and waving had failed, so that the next scene could begin.

On several occasions a nervous mumbling little man appeared. At first I thought he was the producer, but he turned out to be the prompter. He was apparently having difficulty in getting his interpretation of the piece accepted; the actors played their own versions for all they were worth. Sometimes they tried to drive him away, and one man even put out his tongue at him.

By the time the grey light of morning had cast its disillusioning rays into the open theatre building most of the actors had become hoarse. The families began to creep away homewards.

There was no real end, no dramatic climax and no curtain call. The actors just packed up and left the remainder of the audience to sleep on. Only the dark-eyed Gurkha women remained still wide awake. They would be talking about this for months on end when they got home after a long journey to the Himalayas, and so they must not miss the smallest detail.

Even though nobody clapped after the performance it seemed that everyone had had a wonderful night—and particularly the actors. They were not at all offended that so many of the spectators had snored half the time.

With the help of willing hands Reza and I got the car pulled out, and when we arrived home the house-boys had early morning tea ready for us; they didn't appear to be particularly sleepy after their all-night entertainment. Perhaps they were among those who had had a snooze.

The casino owner must also have been pleased that the spectators had managed to rest properly, for when I passed by his establishment later in the forenoon, people were busy playing roulette and bingo for all they were worth.

CHAPTER VII

The Pagoda of the Split Rock

ONE DAY at lunch-time we loaded the jeep with baggage and Burmese, who as usual were very helpful. We now had less than a day's ride before I could photograph the remarkable giraffe women.

"It's almost too easy when you realise how sensational this kind of picture could be."

"Yes, but just wait until you've got your photographs in the bag," replied Reza with a broad grin. "Why do you think I've brought along so many of my friends in the car? Do you really believe that you can photograph them freely, as though they were film stars. Remember, the giraffe women hate cameras, but let's try."

The asthmatic jeep moved off and gave a loud snort every time the ignition fired. What with the condition of the engine and of the road our top speed was only about twenty miles per hour.

At Möng Pai we met some of the remarkable elephant women from the Kayah tribe, with their twelve pounds of steel wire wound round the knees. Here too I could have got some fantastic pictures, but I was out for bigger game. I could always photograph the elephant girls later, if I had any film to spare. So I thought, without suspecting that I should actually have plenty of film left over.

The jeep rumbled on. The earth was red like in Africa, and with its green grass, scattered bushes and termite nests as high as a man, the countryside reminded me of Tanganyika and Rhodesia. In front of us we saw a score of scattered wooden houses, lying half-hidden by the tall crops of millet and maize.

"This is Pekon, and there is your first giraffe woman," said Reza, pointing into the bush. And sure enough there among the shrubs I saw one of these strange women with head and neck sticking up high above the vegetation. But she moved off as soon as she saw me.

As I have said it is only the women of the Padaung race who wear neck-rings; moreover the habit has almost disappeared—it is regarded nowadays as a little old fashioned. At one time the tall necks were not only in fashion, but they also served a rational purpose. It is claimed that the tribe, which came from China, used these rings as a protection against tiger bites. But in their vanity the women have since found out that the golden rings are rather flattering, and the more the better; the result is that their necks have become longer and longer. The head is balanced on the top of a tall spiral and it can't be turned without moving the whole body. Some of these women have come under the influence of the missionaries and have given up many of the old customs, but they cannot take off the neck spiral. Once a giraffe woman, always a giraffe woman, because by itself the neck is no longer able to support the head, but would simply bend over towards the ground, like a branch carrying too much fruit.

Originally the neck-rings were of gold, but this was later replaced by copper. One should not really speak of true rings, but rather of a spiral formed of thick, heavy metal wire, which may be more than a yard long. Sometimes they also wind spirals around their arms and legs.

The neck spirals are a sign of wealth and position and they have of course given the tribe its name: "*padaung*" means "the long necks".

When a girl reaches the age of five, the *bedin-saya* or medicine man decides on the date for a *waso*, a feast at full moon, at which the little girl will have the first spiral put around her neck.

To find out the correct date the *bedin-saya* consults the innards of a chicken. I have come across the same habit in Africa and South America. At first I was puzzled that hens should be used in so many different parts of the world, but then I decided that the medicine men are pretty shrewd; they would not get any material advantage by consulting the internal organs of a mouse or a rat, but they choose a hen because it remains with them after the ceremony.

Once the correct timing has been decided the village is decorated for the feast, at which they make merry on rice wine which has been brewing for the last few weeks.

For many months the little girls have been secretly pulling each others' heads so that they can appear with beautiful long necks. The neck is massaged for a whole day before the spiral is put on, and they also rub in an ointment which makes the skin supple and resilient. (I asked a *bedin-saya* how this ointment was made. At first he was very secretive, but after we had drunk a few glasses of rice wine together he could no longer resist boasting about how cleverly he had concocted it from dog fat, coconut milk and the royal jelly of bees.)

Then for a whole hour after that the little girl's neck is twisted and pulled, and only then are they ready to put on the spiral. The mother stands behind her daughter, pulls her head, lifts the little one up by the chin and twists her neck backwards. On the first occasion the spiral is made about four inches high. They often put in a little cloth under the rings to alleviate the pressure on the collar-bone, and also a thin cushion under the lower jaw. But it is not many days before the girl herself removes both cloth and cushion, for her pride at being accepted into the ranks of the giraffes makes her almost forget the pain.

At a feast twenty-four full moons after this the girl gets an even taller spiral, to replace the original one. The mother again stands behind her daughter, but this time she also has to hold up the head, which the girl is no longer able to support on her stretched and ill-treated neck. A quick look at the girl's neck is enough to tell the medicine man how long the new spiral should be.

On the marriage market the longer the woman's neck the greater the demand. For one thing it is regarded as distinguished in itself to have a long neck. And then it gives the man a better chance to keep his giraffe wife to himself, because the penalty for infidelity is that the medicine man removes the unfaithful wife's spiral. As the neck can no longer support the weight of her head she has to spend the rest of her life lying down—or else permanently supporting her head with her hands. If she let it hang down she would very quickly die of suffocation. It would need a very great love to make this worthwhile. In spite of everything women with normal necks have a somewhat greater chance of surviving an adulterous liaison.

The old Padaung chief, Ahu Ho Gong, smiled readily when we approached him. Yes, he would gladly help us, he said, when I explained that we wanted to film the women.

"Perhaps then you would call them. After all you are their chief."

"No man can be chief over women. I am chief of the men. But women, well! Women only do what they themselves wish," he mumbled and shook his head. "It is the same with women all over the world."

But the giraffe women are perhaps even more independent than their sisters elsewhere. Until about a hundred years ago they ruled the whole tribe, and the little community was distinctly matriarchal. Then followed some savage wars in which a large number of the men were killed, so the standing of the survivors increased. Polygamy was introduced and the men came more into the picture—although evidently not in so far as photography was concerned.

"Haven't you got any daughters that I could photograph? Or sisters?"

"A *myet-hna-gyi* (a top man) cannot tell his *ma-ma-gyi* (elder sister) or his *miy-ma-lay* (younger sister) that they should allow themselves to be photographed. I am indeed the *thugyi* (the village elder) but I only hold sway over the men."

At that moment a man walked by and told us that a child in one of the houses had just died.

"It's just as well this happened before we arrived," remarked Reza. "Otherwise your camera would have been blamed."

"But I haven't even taken a single picture yet," I replied.

"It is quite sufficient that you carry a devil's eye. You must remember that only a few of the Padaungs are Buddhists; most of them are confirmed animists and very superstitious."

"Ask the *thugyi* whether we can be permitted to attend the burial."

"I must say you are an optimist," said Reza. "I am quite certain that they will regard our presence as an evil omen for the soul of the dead child. They will undoubtedly postpone the burial until we have moved on."

This was confirmed by the *thugyi* who told us that the child lay in a flower-decked coffin in the house, where it was being sprinkled with rice wine to strengthen its soul for the long journey. The neighbours had brought gifts which were put in the coffin—rice, tobacco, a couple of roast rats and other delicacies, which would provide sustenance for the dead child on its way to the hereafter. In the evening a flute-player would arrive and they would dance in the house, but nobody would venture out until dawn, for the night was full of spirits who always collected together in such numbers at the time of death that there was almost a queue outside. The woven fans in the entrance were intended to blow these spirits away, and everyone hoped that there would be a strong wind on the burial day so that the fans would work more effectively.

After we had drunk some rice wine and eaten rice cakes I tried to track down a couple of giraffe women—but without success.

"It would be better for you to find the *bedin-saya*, and see whether he couldn't help you," said Reza.

A little boy took us to the old fortune-teller, who only shook his grey head and said that even he did not have the *ausa* (authority) to drive the women out of their hiding-places.

"Now that they know you have a camera," he continued, "they won't be smoked out. But I would gladly read your hand. Perhaps I can find something significant there which would make up for your deficient powers as a conjurer of giraffe women."

"He is very skilful," said Reza. "In fact he is regarded as one of the most competent in the whole of Kayah state."

"Well, let us begin," I said.

The soothsayer grasped my hand, and I reckoned that I could soon show him up. "You travel a lot, and in many countries which are far from your own."

"Yes, to Burma for example."

"You are a good man."

"That is a matter of opinion. Can't you tell me something more specific?"

"You have no faith in astrologers and soothsayers."

"Well, no, so you might as well save yourself the trouble," I said, starting to go. But the man held on fast to my little finger.

"Your line of life is very strong, but you have several times been in great danger."

"Yes, quite possibly—but how?"

"You write books," the man continued imperturbably, "and many people know you."

"Well?"

"You have fought with an anaconda that nearly killed you."

"Damn it! I haven't told that to anyone in Burma." I became a little less restive.

"You have climbed an erupting volcano and seen many head-hunters."

"How do you know that?" I asked.

"You are very obstinate, and it certainly takes a lot to overcome your mistrust. I will give you some advice. Visit the abbot in the Pagoda of the Split Rock. I cannot be sure that he will help you to photograph the giraffe women, because you are not a Buddhist. But if he won't help you nobody else can. Now I am exhausted. If you want to pay me anything, you can put the money in the little box on the table," he said and disappeared behind a curtain.

In spite of everything I was really impressed by him, so I left a rather generous offering in his box. A couple of days later I realised that I had paid more than enough. For I learnt that anyone who knew Burmese could have read all these things in the country's big monthly magazine which had printed a pirated translation of some of my articles on South America, originally published in the United States. After this experience I believed still less in sorcery.

"I know very little about Buddhism," I said to Reza as we travelled back to Loi Kaw. "So I think I should visit the abbot and try to win him over to my side. This will also give me some return for the money I put in the box."

A steep, dark cliff rose high up out of the flat green countryside for no apparent reason, as though planted there by some supernatural joker. But to the Burmese it had plenty of significance. It served quite a definite purpose, for on each of its four peaks towered a white pagoda, and on a small ledge of the cliff there was a Buddhist temple, where lived a highly esteemed abbot.

Taung Gwe, as this monastery on the split cliff is called, is more impregnable than any fortress or any castle of Sleeping Beauty. But the monastery of Taung Gwe houses no Sleeping Beauty, nor indeed is it a defensive position or a hermit's cell, whose monks seek to keep away the outside world.

Taung Gwe is a Buddhist monastery, and so I knew that anyone is welcome, even a foreigner, and even if he belongs to another religion.

A red path, trod by thousands of pilgrim feet, wound its way through the countryside, met other paths with which it joined to form a broad road that led to the cliff. The mud was wet and sticky after the rain, and it squelched under our shoes like melting snow.

There was no temptation to stray, for the sides of the road were lined with shrubs, whose barbed seeds would be difficult to remove from our clothing.

"Do you think there is anyone at home?" I asked an interpreter I had found in the village.

"Oh yes, you can be sure of that. There are several monks living up there; indeed it is regarded as quite a special honour to be a monk in Taung Gwe, which is the most distinguished of our local monasteries."

"How on earth do we get up there? The cliff face is completely perpendicular."

"We get in over there where you see the big brass clock."

The interpreter was quite right. Without any Open Sesame we found a crack in the cliff, in which steps had been cut.

The narrow crevice was crossed by another cleft in the rock and the steps zigzagged steeply upwards. At the entrance to the rift we took off our shoes. Although these hard steps had only been trodden by bare feet they were completely smooth, and so in the steepest parts were the projecting pieces of rock which had been polished by many hands seeking support during the ascent.

Feeling rather breathless we reached a small ledge where three young girls in pink sarongs and thin pale yellow tulle blouses were kneeling to light wax candles in front of a pagoda with a small statue of Buddha.

In other parts of the world this combination of colours would have been rather doubtful, but here it was attractive when seen against the background of green countryside.

When we had recovered our breath we climbed on up several more steps and again stopped for a rest on another ledge. I saw a narrow path that led straight up to the monastery.

"That's fine, we're there at last," I said.

"It is customary for us to go first to the uppermost cliff-top pagoda; this allows the monks to see us and prepare for the visit," said the interpreter.

"In Europe," I replied, "we would get over that by having a waiting-room."

But I did not regret it when we reached the uppermost pagoda, for the view was quite magnificent. To the south lay the flat country, divided up into thousands of fields, their green colours varying according to the growth stage of the rice plants. To the south-east the sun shed a brilliant stripe of silver across the sky which was reflected in the flooded paddy-fields. Northwards was a chain of hills, each crowned by a white pagoda, pointing to heaven as though to remind the Buddhists of their pattern and ideal.

In the west heavy rain clouds hung low over the horizon, but they must have been a hundred or more miles away; there was no need to shelter yet. Far below us, in the centre of a big rift in the cliff stood yet another gigantic statue of Buddha. Its size was obviously more imposing than its æsthetic quality, for it was made of cement and the lines were coarse. Nevertheless it had the same facial expression as all the other figures of Buddha that I had seen. In spite of the soulless way in which the statue was made it expressed by its smile the inner harmony and balance, which is still so characteristic of many Buddhists, and which makes them shrug their shoulders at the haste of the western world. Up there on the cliff-top one had a feeling of being raised high up above the trivialities of daily life. So the monks' visitors do indeed receive a more open welcome than if they had had to sit in a waiting-room.

When we got down to the monastery building itself there was nothing particularly ceremonious. Taung Gwe is a simple teak building clamped on to one of the many rocky ledges. Along a narrow dark passage we came to the monastery kitchen where an attractive young women in a blue *loongyi* was busy preparing a meal over an open fire.

"Are there female staff in the monastery?" I asked inquisitively.

"Oh, no."

"Well, what is that female doing here?"

"Oh, her! That's just a woman who wishes to serve a warm meal to the monks—as a gift to them."

We reached the monastery's largest room by climbing up a creaking staircase, every step serving to warn the abbot of our approach. The floor was covered with patterned linoleum, and the walls, like those of the kitchen, were of coarse boarding. A single step led up to the dais where the abbot was sitting.

As is customary I knelt down with my forehead touching the floor and when I dared to lift my head I saw the well-fed monk, his eyes kind and jovial, watching us from a rickety deck-chair, which constituted his "throne."

"Holy abbot," I said, "I bow to you to show my respect. I would like to say how much I admire the position chosen for your monastery. Even the place itself must surely elevate the mind," and whilst the interpreter was busy translating and telling the abbot all he knew about me I had time to look around.

Behind a curtain at one side I caught a glimpse of two white elephant statues, which had a very puppyish and affectionate look. Wax candles were burning in front of them, and in between them was a sea of flowers; it looked as though they were celebrating a wedding.

"Why do the elephants get flowers?" I whispered to the interpreter.

"The flowers are not for the elephants, but for the Buddha figure at the back," he replied. When my eyes had become accustomed to the gloom I saw that hidden away behind the flowers was a small golden Buddha.

"Well, then, what are the elephants for?" I asked.

"They stand there to honour Buddha; they are sacred white elephants."

"What is our European friend inquiring about?" interrupted the abbot.

"He is wondering about the elephants," replied the interpreter.

"He is quite right to ask. Actually they have nothing to do with Buddhism, but we rather like them and they are doing no harm," continued the monk and then asked:

"Is our friend from Europe a Buddhist? He bowed to me just like one of my own people."

"I am not a Buddhist. We have practically no Buddhists in my country," I replied. "But I have read books on Buddhism, and I am in sympathy with it, as with any other religion which promotes good and fights evil."

The interpreter and the monk had a long parley about this, and I again had a chance to look around the room. By the side of the monk's deck-chair there was a big pile of Burmese cigars, a dozen prickly fruits and some bottles of lemonade. And by the bed, which was on the other side of the elephants, there was a whole pile of similar gifts which visitors had brought him; still more cigars, several packets of lump sugar, bundles of wax candles, dishes of rice, tinned milk, jam, matches. Most of them were small modest offerings, but there was also an up-to-date transistor radio.

"Now tea is served," said the interpreter. I bowed again and politely backed away from the dais. The interpreter just got up, turned his back on the abbot and walked away to sit down on the floor where the tea was served.

I asked in a whisper whether the interpreter thought the abbot would be offended if I took a photograph.

The interpreter laughed loudly: "Offended? No, he loves being photographed. Why on earth should he be offended?"

"Well, I'm sorry, but I have recently been on a journey in Arabia, where it may cost you your life just to own a camera."

The abbot also had a good laugh when this was translated to him. It was a great relief that they could be so cheerful in the monastery, even in the presence of Buddha, and now that I was sure that they would not be offended by my using a camera, I started to take my photographs.

As I was kneeling down to thank him and say good-bye, I came out with my real errand.

"Go on," said the abbot, encouragingly. "You have, I hope, realised by now that I am here to talk to."

"Honoured abbot, I have come to your country to write about the giraffe women, but I have been unsuccessful in my attempts to speak to them or to get permission to photograph them. Can you help me?"

"Is it only the giraffe women that you want to write about?" asked the abbot, a little offended.

"No, I also want to write about the people, about the religion and about the Buddhist monasteries. But the giraffe women are very important. Can you help me?"

The abbot looked at me for a long time and then answered at length and in some detail. I waited patiently for the interpreter to translate. We remained kneeling while the abbot gave me a friendly smile.

"I rather like you and I have heard a good deal about you," my interpreter translated. "The *bedin-saya* who read your hand down in the village has told me that you are a good man. I also knew that you wanted to visit me. Come to me on the day of the full moon, on the *waso* feast, which we hold to celebrate the time that Buddha Gotama first came out of the jungle to talk to his disciples."

"Yes, I'll do that—but what about the giraffe women?"

"They will also be coming," explained the abbot. "And here in the pagoda they will not be afraid that your camera will do them any harm. You should come up with the children's procession."

CHAPTER VIII

The Waso Feast

IT WAS FULL MOON, and with the full moon came the *waso* feast. The long procession of children moved off looking like a multi-coloured python. They all carried fresh flowers and wore them in their hair; they were dressed in their best and most brilliantly coloured clothes. The little girls had their faces covered with a thick layer of powdered bark, their eyebrows painted and their lips red, but nevertheless they were still very child-like. They looked like little princesses, and as they walked along the wet muddy road they seemed to have come from a fairy-tale. They would have been more at home in a fairy palace than on a dirty road in the wild interior of Burma.

Several of the boys wore grown-up felt hats, which gave them a rather precocious appearance. It reminded me of Ecuador and Bolivia and of many places in Africa where the boys also have this peculiar liking for discarded European felt hats.

A little boy walked in front with a bowl of rice; this was for Buddha, as were the flowers.

I followed at the rear of the procession, carrying my camera and wearing a pair of crumpled khaki trousers, spotted with red muddy water. I felt a little out of place, but was nevertheless accepted.

The brilliantly coloured procession looked particularly striking against the dark green countryside, the red sarongs and pale blue and yellow tulle blouses contrasting vividly with the tropical vegetation. The parade went first to a Buddhist school where the children bowed to an old monk. I was not sure whether I ought to go in with them but seeing me hesitate, a little child took me by the hand and led me in: why should I be afraid of Buddha and the nice teacher?

We could now see Taung Gwe, the monastery of the split rock. The slender little arms found new strength to lift up the rice bowls and the flowers; these should preferably be carried high above the head, so that the scent is reserved for Buddha alone.

79

The long procession broke up into small groups under the trees beneath the cliff. Here they took off their sandals and then disappeared as though they had been swallowed up by the dark chasm, and for a moment the whole atmosphere of fairyland had gone. But soon I could see them swarming over a projecting part of the cliff and when they came to a ledge they spread out to the sides like butterflies over a lawn.

Although the sky was grey, the sun shone on the children. The little girls were as slender as porcelain statuettes, as light and ethereal as ballet dancers. Like butterflies which stop in flight to suck nectar, so they all stopped, one or two at a time, in front of the Buddhas on the various ledges, and knelt to light candles. Then they moved on up the cliff and finally into the monastery. Their twittering ceased as they knelt beside each other in front of the abbot, who, as on my previous visit, sat in his deck-chair by the side of Buddha and the two beloved elephants. There were so many flowers to celebrate the *waso* feast that the Buddha was almost smothered by them.

Gifts to Buddha were carried forward, and the chubby monk also received his share—when rain falls on Buddha it also drips on his servants. In actual fact the monk got the lion's share: big bundles of green cigars, tinned milk, biscuits, sugar, orangeade, oranges, bananas and much more, whilst the Buddha over there among the flowers had to make do with a score of wax candles.

Suddenly a white rabbit escaped from the abbot's arms and darted across the floor. The kneeling children were delighted and immediately started a wild chase for it.

I looked anxiously at the abbot. Wouldn't he be angry at all this turmoil in a sacred place? Would he now scold the children and call them to order?

But he just sat there and laughed so heartily that his belly shook. I rather suspected that he had purposely prepared this conjurer's trick with the rabbit. Eventually the animal escaped to a safe place behind the Buddha and the gentle turmoil subsided.

The children left the monastery and lit candles before yet another Buddha, and then set off again down the many steps, were swallowed up by the cliff and disappeared like sparks from a dying firework.

When I returned to the monastery its ruler came up to me and said:
"Now you can safely photograph the Padaung women."

Above: The author receiving a lesson from the abbot. *Below:* Preparations for the author's ordination as a monk. Bat Ears being shaved by "Yul Brynner"

Above: The author in his cell. The low table is covered with notes, films and—cigars. *Below:* the author being ordained as a koo yien

I hurried in and there, in front of the Buddha and the elephants, I saw two really remarkable creatures.

Their necks were even more incredible than I had ever imagined. The head appeared to slope upwards and forwards. Originally the women of this tribe used to have a spiral of two or three rings, but these had at least ten. A dreadful warning of what vanity can lead to! They still make the excuse that the rings protect them against tiger bites, but to me it seemed that, if you met a tiger, you would have a better chance without these rings.

I quickly set up my camera and took a picture. The giraffe women gave a start as the flash went off, and their heads rocked like tall towers in a storm.

"Think only about Buddha," said the abbot gently, and once more the women were at rest.

"Now if you follow the women when they go home you will have a chance to photograph them on the way, and by the time you have reached their houses they will surely have become used to you," he continued. "But come back and tell me how you get on."

As I left the pagoda to follow the giraffe women, I could not help noticing that they had the same rocking gait as the real giraffes which wander over the savannahs of Africa.

As though by magic the women's attitude to me had quite changed. Now that they understood that the abbot had given his consent for me to photograph them, they had become very willing models. And when we reached their homes I was invited to see the latest baby. The neighbouring family, which had already been up to the pagoda earlier in the day, had now changed into working clothes. But they changed back again into their finery, so that I was able to take pictures of both the everyday clothes and the festival dress.

I had a spare film wrapped up in a sheet from one of the Rangoon newspapers, and it had a cinema advertisement with a picture of a young couple kissing each other. One of the giraffe women saw this and asked the interpreter to translate the caption:

> Devenand—hero of the day
> Nutan—girl of your dreams
> Romancing in picturesque Simla.
> Join the crowds at the Roxy—

> Daily 4 shows. Ladies, Mon. Tues. 3 p.m.

Buddha alone knows what the giraffe women thought when they heard this. Possibly they thought we were savages, and that they themselves were far superior, even if they did eat cats and rats. Or perhaps they just could not understand how a man could kiss his beloved without first squatting down.

Whilst my interpreter was talking to the giraffe women I noticed that as they smiled or laughed they were continuously putting out their tongues, so that one could see their betel-red teeth.

"They are much bolder here than they were up at the temple," I said, "they're even putting out their tongues at you."

"That is a sign of friendliness," replied the interpreter. "It is the equivalent of our smiling or paying a compliment."

After I had been some hours with them a young girl arrived who was introduced to me as the daughter of the giraffe woman with the longest neck. This girl, was, however, a modern and had no neck rings. And then I realised that there was some point in the long necks, for to me the mother looked far more elegant and distinguished than her short-necked daughter.

Watching these giraffe women moving about, I was almost afraid that their heads would fall off, for it looked as though each lay loose on top of a long brass tube; it was difficult to believe that they were really connected to the rest of the body. Also the head appeared very small in relation to the body, but this must have been an optical illusion.

Their dress consists of a black skirt and a brown jacket. On festive occasions they wear a white jacket and deck themselves with ear-rings and the necklaces of silver coins which they receive at the neck-stretching feasts.

If, as some say, the long necks are the punishment meted out by the medicine men and the gods for the women's excessive vanity, then it has done little good, for the giraffe women are still extremely vain; they obviously live by the old saying: "one must suffer to be beautiful."

The women's big problem is how to wash these long necks. Actually they do this by slipping a thin damp cloth in between the neck and the spiral, and then pulling it up and down so that it washes the neck and polishes the rings at the same time. It is quiet essential to do this twice a day, otherwise sweat will cause the brass rings to produce verdigris, which could set up sores on the neck.

The Padaungs are very conscious of tribal unity, and the laws which forbid marriage with other tribes are merciless. There are many stories of both men and women Padaungs being buried in the ground up to their necks, because they were unfaithful to their own tribe. These and many strict taboos exist alongside the old animist beliefs. There are still many who worship plants and animals, but the old taboos are disappearing with the advance of Buddhism and Catholicism. The Padaungs are very superstitious and are perhaps more afraid of the dark than any other people in the world, and this is surely a relic of animism. They will never move out at night, and they still hang rattles over the house to frighten away the evil spirits of darkness.

So ended a most eventful day. With due ceremony I too put out my tongue, and then returned to Taung Gwe.

When I came to kneel before the abbot for the third time, to thank him for his help with the giraffe women, he said:

"I will also fulfil your second wish, which is to learn about Buddhism and to photograph life in a monastery. Three monks are waiting outside to take you to Uttararama Monastery, where the old monk Bikkhu Nandavamsa and the abbot Bikkhu Saddhammofrale will take you in hand; perhaps they will make you into a monk."

"Make me a monk?" I said, turning pale.

"Yes, you shall live in the monastery for a time, and learn all that we can teach you about Buddha. And then you will become a monk, be clad in a saffron-yellow robe and have your beard and hair shaved off."

To become a monk, a saffron monk, and have my beard and hair shaved off! This, I felt, was almost too much of a good thing. I had seen these bald-headed monks worshipping Buddha. I had watched them walking barefoot through the village streets, collecting rice for the monastery. They must only look three yards ahead and as far as possible they must avoid speaking. Back in the monastery they may only eat one meal a day—and they have to get up at five o'clock in the morning.

Cautiously I glanced at the abbot. He looked quite determined. Was this a suggestion—or an order? Must I become a monk as thanks for the help he had given me with the giraffe women?

There was something hypnotic about his eyes. I tore myself away from his gaze and looked at the figure of Buddha. The Buddha was smiling.

Why?

I had read quite a number of books on Buddhism, but had I understood them? What did I really know? Perhaps it was reasonable enough that I should acquire a thorough knowledge of monastery life before I began to write about Burma. But to shave off my beard and hair, to enter a monastery. No, that scarcely bore thinking about.

"So now you will be going to the monastery, and you must go now," said the abbot, pointing towards the door.

I looked there, and saw three monks waiting for me—three big, strong monks!

CHAPTER IX

I Enter a Monastery

I looked up again at the abbot. He was still pointing to the door, where the three monks were waiting to take me to Uttararama Monastery. I cast a quick glance at the Buddha behind the two white elephants. No, it wasn't a malicious smile, but rather gentle, with perhaps a touch of fatherly amusement at the corners of the eyes.

The abbot made a slightly impatient gesture. I got up from my knees and walked towards the door.

As we walked down the steps one of the saffron monks went in front of me and the other two behind. When we reached the open country there was one on each side of me and one behind. It was almost like being under arrest. The three men were silent. When I stopped for a moment they too stopped. We walked through the village by the side lanes, avoiding the main street.

Was I obliged to go with them?

Had I been hypnotised by the abbot?

It was three to one, but I am a fast runner and could certainly outstrip them. But where would I run to? And why?

Would the villagers help me—or would they side with their own monks? Perhaps they would let me escape without doing anything about it. But it would be rather silly to leg it around Loi Kaw all alone, particularly if I was not in any danger.

But what would happen to me? I wished that we could meet Reza, but there was not a soul I could talk to, and so I decided that all I could do was to go along with the monks. And I might as well admit it: I am by nature rather an inquisitive fellow and I really did want to take this opportunity to live as a monk in a Buddhist monastery.

When we reached Uttararama I had to take off my shoes and stockings and walk barefoot over the sharp gravel, as becomes an ordinary mortal;

85

the monks kept their sandals on. I wondered whether the thorny mimosas were planted here to remind people to tread warily on holy ground.

In the monastery courtyard there were four small pavilions made of teak; in the centre stood the main monastery building. The Buddha stood in the middle of the central hall, out of which doors led to the individual cells of the monks.

I thought now of my baggage which I had left in the jeep down in the village, but when I was shown to my cell there it was all ready for me. In addition there was a wooden bed without a mattress and lots of chests—perhaps they contained some of the monastery's treasures, but unfortunately they were all padlocked.

There was nothing missing from my baggage, and I began to find my unusual situation both interesting and exciting.

A little later on the abbot of the monastery, Saddhammofrale, came in with an interpreter.

"We are glad that you want to study Buddhism in our monastery. It gives us great pleasure and it will also give pleasure to you; you will come closer to Nirvana."

"Your Reverence need not thank me, for I have always wanted to know something about Buddhism," I murmured solemnly, but I still did not feel quite at ease.

"Buddha shows us the right way, but he does not carry us along it: you must achieve the end by yourself. Buddha never says 'thou shalt'. Buddhism is a voluntary affair. It depends on your own disposition, on your own free will, on whether you want to get to know the ways of Buddha."

I thought this sounded very reassuring and asked, perhaps a little too eagerly:

"Can I leave when I want to?"

"Yes, you can, but now that you are here we should be very sorry if you left before you became a *koo yien*. And you would not want to make us unhappy."

"No, of course not, Your Reverence," I replied, without really knowing what a *koo yien* was.

When the abbot had left I asked the interpreter how long it would take to become a *koo yien*.

"It can be done in about a year," he replied. "But there are some who take three or four years." I had not thought of spending all that time on it, but this I did not mention.

That night I lay on my hard bed and considered the problem. Now that I knew it was quite voluntary I really wanted to stay some time in the monastery and to study its life. And if I could really accept the teaching of Buddha, then I could indeed envisage myself becoming a *koo yien* as the first grade monks are called—at any rate for a time. I owed it to myself and to my readers to go into the facts properly. But a whole year! What would my wife say about being married to a monk for so long? I could not really see any solution to the problem. It would need a prodigy to get through the training in a month or two.

Then suddenly I was wide awake with a new idea. My Minifon, my miniature tape-recorder, which I sometimes use when it is too difficult to take notes, surely it could help me.

The next morning I met the abbot and told him I had been thinking it all over, and unfortunately the time at my disposal was very limited. Could I nevertheless try to see how far I could get in the time available?

"My friend, we shall help you as much as we can. We will gladly take it in turns to teach you from morn to night, but there are many, many things to learn. And if you are to remember them you must repeat them again and again."

"I have a 'limpet' brain. When I hear something once it sticks there," I replied, a little arrogantly.

And that is how I started on my lightning course in Buddhism.

I was busy settling into my cell, although still a little bewildered at the speed with which things were happening, when a little *koo yien* came in without knocking on the door. He pointed first at me and then at the abbot's house, and so I knew that my first lesson was about to begin.

Saddhammofrale lived in a modest little timber house with a rusty corrugated iron roof. The original and more imposing residence was burnt down about twenty years ago. His office served also as living-room, class-room and study. An unpretentious table was strewn with books and papers; there was no chair by the table for the abbot always sat on the floor to write. And for this he had an additional small round table with legs only ten or eleven inches high.

His little altar to Buddha stood on a plain pinewood table with a plastic cloth. The Buddha was surrounded by vases and jam-jars filled with fresh flowers. There was also an alarm clock which helped the abbot when he had a class; it rang when the hour was up. The floor was covered with woven matting.

When I arrived he had just finished with a class of schoolchildren, who ran from the class-room a little less boisterously than some school pupils in other parts of the world—perhaps the abbot had given them strict instructions to behave properly and to set the new boy a good example.

When I had knelt to him the abbot indicated with a movement of his arm that I should sit down on the floor. The interpreter had not yet arrived, so we sat and smiled at each other, but without feeling self-conscious. For monks there is never any hurry.

Outside the birds were singing and the plants were bursting in through the windows. On one of the branches I saw a bread-fruit, just waiting for a hungry boy. When the interpreter appeared I was given my basic time-table:

5 a.m.	When the big gong sounds, everyone goes in to kneel before the Buddha.
6. a.m.	A cup of smoked tea is served, without sugar.
7-9.30 a.m.	Instruction
10-11 a.m.	Bath
11-12 noon	The only meal of the day: a portion of rice.
noon-1 p.m.	Rest or work
1-4 p.m.	Instruction or Homework
4-5 p.m.	Homework
5-6 p.m.	Instruction
6 p.m.	Good night to Buddha

After this there might be an evening walk, but only if permission had been given, and you always had to be back in the monastery by 8 p.m. at the latest.

During the first lessons we went through this time-table in detail. The abbot explained that they got up at such an ungodly hour in order to set a good example to the villagers, who would find it easier to rise at six, if they knew that the monks had already been up and about for a whole hour.

"In the morning when you kneel before the Buddha for ten minutes you must never pray or in general wish for anything. You must only think about Buddha's good deeds, his good example, and at the same time realise that you yourself must set a good example to others."

Above: A 'family group' with the author in the centre, surrounded by monks and sponsors. *Left:* Abbot Saddhammofrale of Uttararama Monastery. *Centre:* "Yul Brynner", the author's neighbour in the monastery. *Right:* The author, a frog's eye view

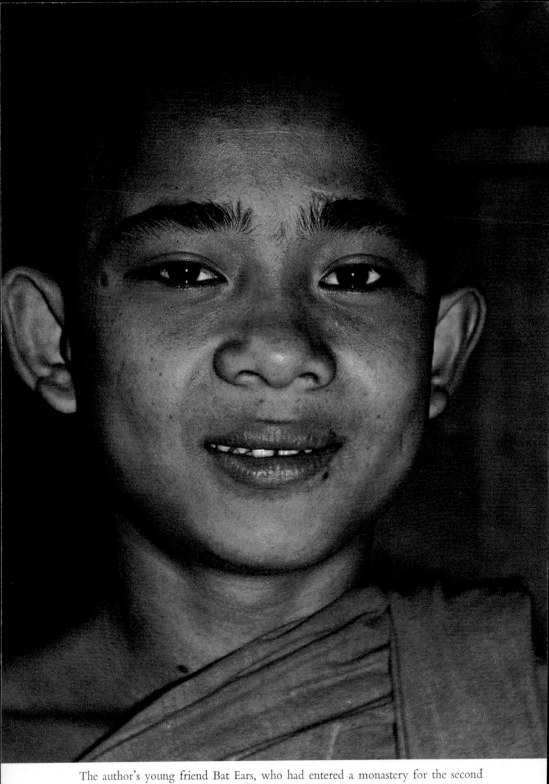

The author's young friend Bat Ears, who had entered a monastery for the second time, to revise his understanding of the true Buddhism

Above: Whilst little girls kneel in respect, the shaven Danish monk collects a handful of rice from each of Loi Kaw's grateful inhabitants. Unfortunately the road had been recently covered with fresh sharp gravel. *Below:* Bat Ears presents a tray of food to Buddha

The two elephants at Taung Gwe Monastery, looking like outsize pets, rather
dominated the little statue of Buddha in the background

"Do you take sugar in your tea?" continued the abbot.

"Yes, I usually do, but I can easily do without it," I replied, in astonishment.

"That's excellent, because at six o'clock we get a cup which we drink without sugar, so that it shall not be regarded as a stimulant. After that we will begin our lessons; I will lecture to you and discuss Buddhism until about ten o'clock, when you can take a bath."

"Can I go for a swim in the lake?" I asked innocently, but realised immediately that this question had not been well received.

"A monk does not play. He only takes a bath to keep clean. We have a small bath-house over in the corner of the courtyard, where all the flowers are. When a monk takes a bath he must always remember to keep on his yellow *tchingan*."

"Why is that?" I asked in amazement.

The interpreter began his own private explanation, but the abbot interrupted and the interpreter again translated:

"It serves two practical purposes: the first is that the sweat will be rubbed off the body by the *tchingan*, and the second is that there will be no risk that a woman should see a naked monk and get the idea of leading him into temptation. When you change from the wet to the dry *tchingan* you must put on the dry one before you let the wet one fall."

The abbot must have seen me smiling, for he too smiled and said:

"You may smile at these rules, but you must follow them when you become a *koo yien*. There is scarcely any reason to smile at the next rule: we have a modest meal at eleven o'clock and then eat nothing else for the rest of the day."

"Is it then sinful to eat?" I asked, thinking of the fleshpots back at home.

"No, certainly not, but it is not good to eat too much; it would only give offence, particularly since we receive our food as an offering. But a handful of rice is worth almost nothing, it is a symbolic gift which is not much more expensive than the flowers people sometimes present to us. During the afternoon you can sit in your cell and write down what I have told you, and you can work on your book about our country and our philosophy. And if you feel the need you can come and talk to me."

Finally the abbot reiterated:

"You must remember never to leave the monastery without permission. But every evening at sunset I will walk with you for an hour, so that you can get some exercise."

At first the abbot had insisted that I should note down the time-table, but he soon realised that my little Minifon could repeat everything and so I was excused from writing. Thanks to the same little gadget the abbot covered far more ground in each lesson than he had reckoned on. (Here I should mention that in some places the statements made by my charming tutor may appear somewhat naïve. This is, of course, due to the simplified translations by the interpreter; my teacher must certainly have expressed himself according to the best philosophical usage.)

"Never before in the history of Kayah state has a European become a monk, but you have great gifts, my son, and these will carry you through," said the abbot after the first few lessons, and I was very proud —particularly on behalf of my Minifon.

Here are some of the things I learnt.

Buddhism is five hundred years older than Christianity, and to-day it has several hundred million adherents. Just as the doctrines of Christianity were first written after the death of Jesus, so also were the tenets of Buddhism recorded after the death of Buddha, indeed some three to four hundred years later. They were written in Pali, the sacred language of Buddhism, and they contain rules for the monastic life and also sermons, which often remind one of the parables of Jesus. In addition they contain the legend of the birth and life of Buddha and tell about the many hundreds of living forms that a future Buddha must experience before his final birth. He must live now as a man, or as a more or less noble animal. (Among the animals the vegetarians such as elephants or hares are regarded as superior to the beasts of prey; these are reckoned inferior because they kill.) When in the course of his evolutionary progress he is reborn as a man, it will be in widely different situations in life—anything from a prince to a herdsman. When a man is reborn as a Buddha it means that he has reached a climax in his development, above all in his spiritual development.

When Buddhism speaks of rebirth, there is no question of a transmigration of souls, but rather an evolutionary process—almost in the Darwinian sense—just as one can imagine the physical evolution of, for example, a race of animals.

Buddhism has gradually split into different sects. The orthodox form, *theravada* (now called *hinayana*), which my teacher professed, has not altered much since the beginning. Nowadays its adherents are found particularly in Ceylon, Burma, Thailand, Cambodia and Laos.

Mahayana has become widespread in the other Far Eastern countries, particularly Japan and China. Lamaism is still found in Tibet and was important in Mongolia until the advent of Communism. Finally there is Zen Buddhism which originated in Japan and has become rather fashionable in Europe and America during recent decades.

Mahayana differs to some extent from the original Buddhism in that it almost regards Buddha as a god, to whom a man may pray. Furthermore *Mahayana* also recognises earlier Buddhas, known as Bodhisattvas, which can help you on your way to the final goal. It is on this point, in particular, that *Mahayana* clashes with orthodox Buddhism, which says very definitely that there is no short cut to salvation, but that everyone gets the reward he deserves, that everyone is the master of his own destiny.

Lamaism has deviated so much from the original Buddhism and has annexed so much necromancy and other magic rites that it no longer has much in common with the teaching of Buddha.

Zen Buddhism is, as the Zen experts themselves admit, very difficult to define; but if our European Zen Buddhists really had a chance to study the original Buddhism I believe that many would find it preferable.

Most religions have more or less strict rules about what you should believe and how you should behave, but Buddhism does not have these. There is no compulsion and no condemnation if you fail to follow some of the rules. It is essentially based on a logical sequence: that which does good is good, and that which does evil is evil and, in the eyes of eternity, everyone gets his due rewards.

An act is evil if it binds you to material existence or makes you a slave to earthly possessions, and an act is good if it emancipates. Buddha's teaching is therefore the opposite of materialism. Moreover Buddha says that if you are at peace with yourself then you have no need of his guidance: he compares himself with a doctor who comes when a sick man wishes to get better, or with a nursemaid who looks after a child. The holy man will watch over the monk when he is young and immature, when he is still a *koo yien*. Later when the young man has learned to stand on his own feet, he must look after himself.

Buddha believes in a moral code for the universe, a code of behaviour, but not in a higher god as creator or lord. He does not take exception to other religions nor does he oppose them. He says that anyone can be happy in his own beliefs if his deeds are what they ought to be, but naturally Buddhists think that those who follow the example of Buddha will find the best way to salvation.

Buddha speaks against desire, but he is neither so passive nor so negative as many have suggested, usually through a lack of understanding. Although it is commonly thought that Buddhism is passive I believe that one could safely maintain that it is more active than Christianity. For the Christian can give up the struggle and only has to pray and put his problems into the hands of God, whereas Buddha preaches that one good deed is more valuable than a thousand prayers. Like Christ he commends mercy. He says that, just as a mother risks her life to defend her child, so each one of us should manifest an infinite unselfishness towards his neighbours—and Buddha also includes the animals amongst man's "neighbours." This selflessness is known as *metta*, and Buddha tells his monks that *metta* is much more valuable than piety. One should tend the sick and help those in need.

There is a story that Buddha once came to a monastery where there was a monk whose illness was so repulsive that no one would nurse him. But Buddha went in and nursed him and remained with him several days, and then charged the monks with his care. Such an act of mercy brings to mind the Good Samaritan, with Buddha himself as the Samaritan.

Buddhism does not recognise the concept of a soul. The Hindus and the ancient Egyptians avoid killing animals because they believe that an ancestor may have assumed the form of the animal. The Buddhists refrain from killing because they have a respect for life itself. And that which is reborn is not an abstract, indefinable soul, but a heritage, which is passed to the children, a heritage which they in turn can improve or diminish before they pass it on to their own children.

For those interested in getting a positive and accurate insight into Buddhism I would recommend especially Narada Thera's *Buddhism in a Nutshell*. Once familiar with this book the reader can turn to others on the subject, and here I would refer him to the bibliography at the end of this book.

During my stay in Uttararama Monastery nobody once tried to persuade me, or to put pressure on me; nobody once spoke disparagingly about my own or any other religion. I was treated as a guest who had, of his own free will and out of his interest in the subject, come to learn about the teachings of Buddha, and everyone did his best to forward my studies. The coercion which I expected and feared when I moved into the monastery existed only in my own imagination.

At any time during my stay in the monastery I could have packed my bags and gone on my way. But the long talks I had with Sadd-hammofrale increased my interest in Buddhism, which seemed to be agreeably free of some ideas in Christian teaching which I cannot accept. For example, I have always felt myself extraordinarily repulsed by the Christian doctrine that condemns even those who have never heard the gospel to eternal weeping and gnashing of teeth. I believe that many of the natives I have lived amongst, who have never had a chance to learn about Christianity, are better men, more high-minded and in the best sense more moral than the average so-called Christian.

Christianity speaks of an original sin, from which we must be saved; this Buddhism does not recognise. And Christianity, which is often called "the Religion of Love" teaches of a last judgment after death. According to Buddhist thinking it is rather uncharitable to commit the millions who have never had the chance to hear the word of God to eternal suffering.

Aldous Huxley has written somewhere that alone among all the great religions of the world Buddhism has advanced without persecution, censure or inquisition. And Lord Russell wrote: "We are told that the world was created by a god, who is both good and almighty. Before he created the world he foresaw all the suffering and misery that it would contain. He is therefore responsible for it all. It is useless to argue that the world's misery is due to sin. If God knew beforehand the sins that mankind would commit, then he was clearly responsible for the conse-quences of all these sins, when he decided to create man."

Buddhism allows man to use his reason, and in contrast with Christianity it actually exhorts him to do so, and therefore I—and many like me—maintain that Buddhism is more a philosophy than a religion. Buddha and his good thoughts have become an ideal for me. I admire him and feel myself in debt to him just as I am to other good men and other great thoughts. But if I find anything in Buddhist teaching that I cannot accept, I reserve to myself the right to follow my own judgment. This Buddha would have approved.

As lesson followed lesson, I succeeded in filtering out a number of Buddhist legends and myths which seemed rather preposterous to a

Westerner, and the true Buddhist philosophy began to appear in a clearer light.

The highest peak which a Buddhist can reach is Nirvana, a form of eternal bliss which is very difficult to define. Nirvana means extinction, but the word is easily misunderstood, for it should not, as often happens, be regarded as complete effacement. Perhaps it would be more accurate to say that Nirvana denotes the obliteration of earthly desires. Man attains Nirvana when he has written off all material standards.

Nirvana is not a reward for good deeds—any more than rebirth as a lesser being is a punishment. Nirvana is a consequence, an impartial and dispassionate, but invariable result of the law of causality.

In Buddhism the chain of causality is not broken by death. Things started during a man's lifetime still go on, and death makes no change.

As I have said, Buddhism does not teach about a migration of souls, but rather about a destiny, a karma, which governs the total relationship between beings living at different times. Over æons of time, life has evolved from unicellular creatures, through amœba, fishes, and birds, until man appeared as, at present, the last result of an endless series of causal relations. We are the product of earlier existences, and, both physically and mentally, the links in a chain of existence which will continue into eternity.

The karma, or evolution, does not stop because an individual man dies, but there is continuity. All physical and moral life in the world must be regarded as parts of a great coherent whole. Because of cause and effect we are all therefore dependent upon each other. This is one of the reasons why we must not do harm to others, and at the same time must strive not to be influenced by the way our fellow-men behave towards us.

If our neighbour enriches himself at our expense or is malicious towards us, then it is worse for him because he thereby binds himself more firmly to material things, and so to the wheel of suffering. If we repay evil with evil, then we too become bound to the same wheel. But if we avoid being infected by our neighbour's maliciousness and reply to it with invariable gentleness, then we shall come a step nearer to Nirvana. An understanding of Nirvana cannot, according to Buddha himself, be reached by contemplation alone, although one can, through Buddha's instructions, get some small idea of what Nirvana means. Buddha says that he who clings to riches would do better to cast them away rather than let them poison his mind. But if he uses his wealth rightly then he can do something for the welfare of his fellow-men. Wealth and power and honour are not evil in themselves, unless a man is enslaved by them.

It is difficult for a European to accept the great poverty of the East. For the Buddhist it is somewhat easier and they have often been criticised for this. But, taken overall, Buddhists do not regard material things as a yardstick for happiness: a poor man, or one who suffers, may be spiritually richer than a millionaire. This explains their whole attitude.

Jesus also set the poor man above the rich, so it is curious that Christianity has flourished as it has in money-conscious Europe and North America.

Whereas Buddhism's demands or ideals are stricter than those of Christianity, and the responsibility put upon the individual is greater, the teaching of Buddha is milder in that he teaches the continuity of life, so that no one stands in judgment on a man—only his own deeds. And if he lives another thousand lives he always has the possibility to fight again and again against desire, and finally to enter into Nirvana, the Buddhists' heaven, where Buddha embodies a union of the two ideals of righteousness and love.

In the West, Christianity seems to be stifled by those very worldly things against which it is always preaching. But in the East, a man's ambitions are not set so much on accumulating wealth but rather on bringing the inner life into a kind of philosophical harmony with the outside world.

As I have said Buddhism is more a philosophy than a religion. There is no formal worship, but a Buddhist kneels before the figure of Buddha and thinks about his good example; this implies no greater devotion than if a man from the Western world were to stop in front of a statue of Plato or Socrates, in honour of the thoughts that these philosophers have bequeathed to us. The fact that Buddhism is primarily a philosophy of life is surely one of the reasons why it has never produced fanatics, has never started a religious war and has only sent forth a very small number of missionaries. It would not dream of disseminating the thoughts of Buddha by force and the sword, and still less of buying "souls" with knives, beads and brilliantly coloured cottons, as Christian missionaries have done for centuries.

The German philosopher Oswald Spengler has written on the relation between western and eastern morals as a function of their respective religions or philosophies. He affirms that in Western Europe we all live under the influence of a huge optical illusion. Everyone wants something from someone else. The words "thou shalt" are implicit in the conviction that something actually can and should be altered, shaped and ordered. The belief that this is possible, and that man has the right to do it, is immutable. Here it is ordered; obedience is demanded. This is what we mean by moral. In the Western ethic everything is direction, the demand for power, for actions willed into the remote future. Luther and Nietzsche, popes and Darwinians, socialists and Jesuits are all in it together. Their ethics claim to be of a general and lasting validity . . . He who thinks or teaches anything else is a sinner, a renegade, an enemy who must be fought without mercy. Mankind shall: the State shall: the community shall. For us this is the only true ethic. But it was otherwise in India, in China, and in the ancient world. Buddha offered a model, Epicurus gave good counsel; their ethic is a high but voluntary one.

To me, it is strange that the so-called democratic western world follows such an undemocratic, despotic ethic, which, compared with Buddhism, is really a kind of dictatorship.

Quite recently some of the leading Buddhists in Ceylon decided that the time had come for the world to have a better chance to get to know about the philosophy of Buddhism, and they have begun to train preachers, who will travel to all parts of the world.

One day when I was sitting in my cell, digesting one of Saddhammofrale's lessons, the door opened suddenly:

"So you also want to become a *koo yien*! Welcome, welcome," shouted Bat Ears with an enthusiasm which was rather out of place in a dignified monk, and stormed into my cell in a scarcely monastic way.

"Well, yes," I replied. "At any rate I am spending a little time studying in the monastery."

"Now I understand better why you asked me so much about Buddhism when we were sailing down the Pilu," he said, and then told me how glad he was to see me again, and how nice it was to have me living in the monastery.

When we were together on the river he had had short, black hair; now he was wearing the yellow robe, and his head had been shaved all over, and his ears seemed more than ever like little wings; he also seemed much more mature. At the same time he had not lost his sense of humour, and every time he smiled I recognised the boy from the boat,

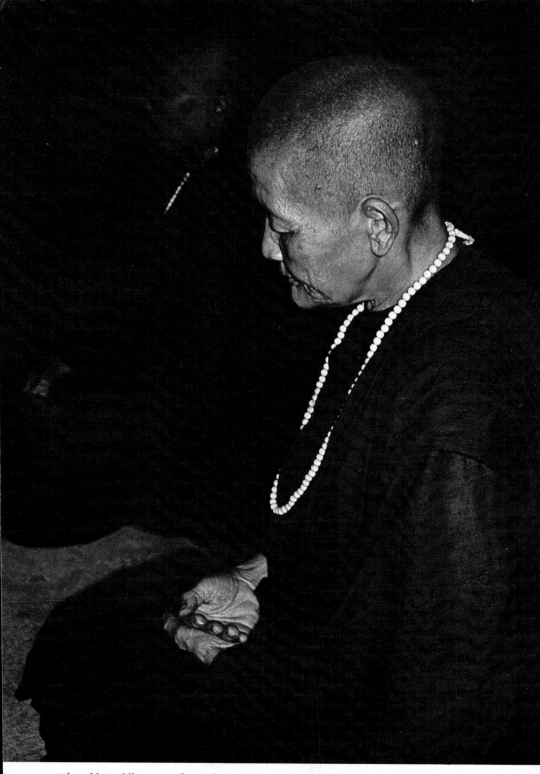

The old Buddhist nun from the kitchen, in deep meditation. The white pearl
necklace is not worn as jewellery, but as a prayer chain, which helps her to recall
Buddha's good deeds

Outside Bangkok itself the canals act both as main streets and as market-places

his mouth almost filling the whole of his face and exposing his big white teeth.

"I will try to get transferred to this monastery," he said, and sure enough that evening he called again, beaming with joy, and told me that he had got permission to move from Taung Gwe, where he had originally been enrolled.

"When you become a *koo yien* you will be my younger brother," he said, and I realised that it is seniority and not age that counts.

So Bat Ears moved into the next cell, and we saw a lot of each other. The many small incidents and conversations I had with him and the abbot, together with what I already knew about Buddha, allowed me to build up a mosaic picture of Buddhism, which became more and more important to me as time went on.

At first the abbot had looked as serious as I myself felt, but now he beamed all over his face whenever we met. And when he was telling me about Buddha's virtues and defining the words omniscient, almighty, and so on, it was easy for me to follow, for these were concepts which Christianity may well have acquired from Buddhism, and so I knew about them. Scholars, however, maintain that Christianity arose quite independently of Buddhism, although there are a surprising number of parallels.

The whole of Loi Kaw was seething with talk about the European pupil in Uttararama Monastery, the pupil with the wonderful brain. They were magnanimous enough to ignore the fact that this brain sat in my right hip-pocket, that it was called Minifon, and that it reproduced both Burmese and the sacred Pali tongue, in fact every sneeze from my teacher's nose. I was delighted too that the little microphone, which hung around my neck, acted as a loudspeaker; thanks to it I was able to reproduce the longest and most difficult passages—as long as I got the right end of the tape.

And then one day the abbot came and told me that the date of my ordination must be postponed for one week, because there was a big stir among the leading families in the town. They wanted to give a big feast for me in connection with the ceremony.

"People are so pleased that you are going to become a monk," said the abbot, "and they are so full of admiration that you should want to keep our commandments. So long as you are a monk you *must* keep to the ways of Buddha, although ordinary people regard most of these rules only as something to be aimed at. They try just to obey the first four or five of the ten commandments, but you yourself must promise to obey them all when you are ordained as a monk of the first grade."

These are the ten commandments:

Thou shalt not kill men or animals.

Thou shalt not steal or dishonestly acquire anything which is not thine.

Thou shalt not lie or in any way speak falsehoods.

Thou shalt not commit adultery.

Thou shalt not drink alcohol.

Thou shalt not eat after the hour of noon.

Thou shalt not take part in amusements of any kind.

Thou shalt not use hair oil, scent or any other form of cosmetic.

Thou shalt not sit in any easy-chair or use a comfortable bed.

Thou shalt not own money or jewellery.

"These are the first ten commandments," said the abbot, "and if you become a monk of the second grade there are a further twenty-seven commandments. But first of all let us see how you manage to keep the ten," he added, with a smile.

CHAPTER X

Life as a Koo Yien

THE TIME for my ordination was fast approaching and I was busy
writing and learning the remaining sayings in the sacred tongue, for in
two days' time I was to become a *koo yien*, or *seameni*, as it is called in
Pali.

At first I tried to divide my time equally between Buddha and the
journal, which would later be used as a basis for this book, but I soon
became increasingly interested in what the abbot taught me. It was not
only "good copy," but also worthwhile in its own right. Buddhism
from the inside! Life in a monastery! Why does Buddha smile? There
were indeed plenty of interesting topics, not only for a book, but also
for personal reflection.

The more I learned about Buddhism the more it seemed to me that
there was a place for its ideas in the cynical materialism of the western
world, to combat our worst evils: competition for social prestige, the
economic rat-race, the political press and all the stress that afflicts the
modern world. If Buddhism was introduced everywhere war would be
theoretically impossible. It is true that Buddhism has not completely
managed to prevent wars and civil wars, but unlike Christianity it has
never been the pretext or excuse for any war.

"I really am surprised that you have never pressed Buddhism at the
expense of Christianity. You well know that I come from a Christian
country," I said one day to the abbot.

"I have said explicitly that we consider prayers as such to be worthless,
and that it is deeds that count. If you are a bad man, it will not help
you to pray; you ought on the other hand to try and behave in the right
way. If you are a good man you don't need to pray. One good deed is
better than thousands of prayers," he reiterated. "It is true that the
Lamaists have prayer-wheels, but we regard these as worthless. I do not
criticise anyone, for nobody becomes better by criticising others. I only
want to show you Buddha's way."

99

"So Buddhists do not therefore regard Christianity as a rival, even though the Christian tries to win converts from among the Buddhists?"

"As I have said before, there are many ways," replied the abbot pateintly. "And Christianity is only one of them. Therefore our country supports the Christian mission work, even though we believe that you will reach the goal more quickly if you follow Buddha."

"And a Buddhist does not recognise original sin and salvation," I said.

"No," replied the abbot. "As I have told you many times the Buddhist view is that every man is the architect of his own destiny. Nor do we recognise saints as the Catholics do. It is exclusively the sum total of a man's own good and less good deeds that determines his fate."

"Why are there no real Buddhist missionaries?" I asked.

"Because if a man wants to follow Buddha he must do so of his own free will, and this would not be so if we tried to impose our views on him. We do, however, have a few wandering preachers who give those who wish it a chance to learn about Buddha."

Thanks to my Minifon the lessons were brief and effective, and when I played back the tapes my little typewriter was kept very busy. The abbot often used to pop his head in at the door of my cell and smile encouragingly when he saw how hard I was working.

On my very first day he had given permission for me to have a long-legged table and chair in my cell, so that I could work as I was accustomed to. But I declined. I did not want privileges, so I sat on the floor like the other monks.

I did however come to regret this decision, but now it was too late. I became very sore on that part of me that was closest to the floor for most of the day, and my back ached. Normally I sit in an arm-chair and dictate, but here I had to hammer away on the typewriter myself, and from a very awkward position.

Sometimes when I looked up from the machine there would be some young spectators who had quietly sneaked in to see what I was up to. Among them were two little orphan girls, whom the monastery had adopted. They looked only four or five years old, but were probably seven or eight. They walked around hand in hand, almost as though they had grown together. Always beautifully clean, they would sit on the floor in a corner and listen to the lesson or else play around on the sharp gravel outside like a couple of chickens that had escaped from the mother hen. Apart from the two old women in the kitchen, there was apparently nobody who took much notice of them, but nevertheless they appeared to be content with their fate.

They were so inordinately inquisitive that they would creep in to me several times a day. However they were so shy that if I just looked up or tried to give them a photograph, they would rush out of my cell into the big hall of Buddha, down the monastery steps, over the court-yard, and into the kitchen to the old women. And when I looked up from my machine an hour or two later there they would be again, close to the door and pressed tight against the wall—and still hand in hand. By now I had learned a smattering of Burmese and if I spoke to the girls without looking at them they usually gave a little chirping answer before they again fled.

Bat Ears also used to come and visit me. He was very welcome, for he just sat down and puffed away at a big cigar—and he usually had far more with him than he could manage to smoke. He sat there like a real connoisseur, fanatically watching the big blue clouds of smoke as they spread out into the cell.

I was glad that it was not sinful in the eyes of Buddha to have a smoke. But unfortunately the cigars became very frayed and the burning flakes had a tendency to fall into your lap; you had to sit up with a straight back when you smoked. It would not do to lean back in the deck-chair, which formed part of the inventory of my Spartan cell, and in which I rested between the chapters, for then the sparks would quickly burn a hole in your *tchingan*.

There was one *koo yien*, whom I called Yul Brynner; he had dark eyes and a domed head. He was also a welcome guest who could enjoy a good cigar without disturbing people at work.

On the other hand I was always a little nervous when the thin sickly Seamihu came in. For one thing he expected the other *koo yien*, who might only be a few years his junior, to kneel respectfully in front of him. (Strictly speaking this was quite correct, but in practice it was almost never done between monks of about the same seniority.) And as an ordinary mortal I too should have knelt to him even though he was six years younger than me, but he had difficulty in explaining this to me —in such situations the language barrier is almost insuperable!

But the worst thing about Seamihu was that he was ambitious to instruct me in both Burmese and Pali. And strangely enough he could always sense when Yul Brynner, Bat Ears and I were having a pleasant break and a nice quiet smoke. Eventually I got him to sit by himself and speak into my tape recorder; then I could listen to it when I felt in the mood. It was very amusing to see him sit down and talk so piously and enthusiastically into the little microphone.

The abbot pointed out time after time that Buddhism puts no pressure on anyone.

"Buddhism gives you the ideals, but it does not give you definite rules of conduct. Buddhism lays the whole responsibility on your own conscience. You should try to improve yourself, not for the sake of the law but for your own sake. You must be humble and industrious and do good deeds."

"According to the first commandment I must not kill—why then may I eat meat?" I asked.

"Yes," answered the abbot. "Life is sacred, and as a monk you may not kill, but you may certainly eat meat, as long as you have not seen the animal being killed or have been the cause of its death."

"Well," I said. "Does that mean that butchers and fishermen are bad Buddhists?"

"They are not monks, and so do not need to pay such strict attention to the commandment. But even if they feel compelled to undertake necessary slaughter, they can still hold to the ideal of: thou shalt not kill."

"Slaughter is then only 'necessary' in so far as anyone is prepared to eat the slaughtered animal."

To this the abbot made no reply.

"And what do you think about those who hunt for pleasure?" I asked.

"Well," he replied. "From the Buddhist viewpoint it is definitely not a good thing to hunt animals for your own pleasure, but remember that it is not for us to judge, nor is it our duty to add up life's balance sheet. I can only say that if you improve yourself you will come closer to being reborn in Nirvana or Paradise, or whatever you prefer to call it. And contrariwise you will be farther away from it if you do something that is wrong."

The conversation switched to rebirth, and the abbot said that a bad man may be reborn as a lower being, for example a cow or worst of all a beast of prey. This I found a little difficult to follow.

"Abbot, it is difficult for me to believe that a man can be reborn as an animal. This being so can I still become a *koo yien*?"

"You do not need to have exactly the same beliefs as the rest of us.

But can you, quite briefly, tell me what you believe about a man's good and bad deeds?"

"I believe that a man's good deeds will be an advantage to him in the present life or in the next, and that a kind of justice also probably exists with regard to his wicked deeds."

"That is good, clear thinking," said the abbot, as we continued.

"If by accident you should happen to tread on an ant, this will not be considered a sin, because the important thing is whether your intentions are good or bad," continued the abbot and he illustrated his thoughts with many other examples.

During the final days the lessons became increasingly shorter. I suppose the abbot had realised that there was no point in repeating the same thing again and again, with only formal variations (as certain Christian priests do), when the interpreter's vocabulary was only sufficient to express the gist of the matter. Also the interpreter often had difficulty in keeping awake. Sometimes I had the feeling that he did not really understand anything of what he was translating.

We always sat on the floor during these conversations. My legs went to sleep and I tottered when I had to stand up, but as usual the lovely green cigars fully compensated for any temporary discomfort.

The day before my ordination the lessons were interrupted in a pleasant way. A charming old lady, from the town's aristocracy, came in to ask if I would object if she and two friends gave the feast for me. She had an intelligent face, friendly eyes and a beautiful smile—funnily enough she reminded me of a Douanier Rousseau portrait. She was called Daw Sao Mya and she arrived with two men, U Win Myint and U Kyaw Pe, and they all three wanted to thank me and support me in my wish to become a *koo yien*.

The three friends sat down on the ground, and the abbot continued his instruction quite unaffected by their presence.

"During the ceremony your hair and beard will be shaved off, and when they fall you can think that this symbolises the decay of the body. To-day you are proud of your hair and beard, but to-morrow they will be like a hair that you find in your food; you will loathe them. And when the body is dead it, too, is only dust. Now remember that you must never pray to Buddha for anything. When you kneel before Buddha you should think about his good deeds and his good example. Buddha does not save us, he has just left us his good example, and our conscience must decide whether we follow it and improve ourselves. And when you become a *koo yien*, you yourself must set a good example. So you must obey the ten commandments I have already given you, and continue to do so until you take off your robe."

My last lesson before becoming a *koo yien* was finished. I stood in my cell and gazed out over the countryside. There was a wonderful view from the monastery. To the west I could see the meandering River Pilu, with its bridges and swarms of human beings. To the north lay the little town, its inhabitants going about their daily tasks—I was already beginning to feel detached from the world—and to the east lay the lovely lake, encircled by a forest of blue water hyacinths. Behind the lake some enormous kapok trees grew on the slope, and behind them again a string of hills, which looked blue in the distance. From the steps of the monastery, I could see as many as fifteen pagodas, set on top of each peak in the area; highest of all was the Pagoda of the Split Rock, Taung Gwe, with its four stupas.

To the south there were big meadows, where herds of water buffalo were grazing. It is forbidden to kill them, and whether or not you are a Buddhist, this is common sense, because the country has had a shortage of draught beasts ever since the brutal Japanese invasion during the last war. Farther away to the south there were mountain chains—not steep and rugged, but low and friendly like the people of Burma.

What have you really let yourself in for? I asked myself. Can you do what you're going to do with a clear conscience? Well, I thought I could, because in my view the basic tenets of Buddhism are either identical with, or better than, those of Christianity. And from the human and ethical viewpoint it can only be good to try and forget for a time the turmoil of the outside world and have peace to think about life.

Darkness fell quickly, and the cicadas started to sing. Somebody was hammering away on a giant gong shaped like a half-moon, and each beat made such a deafening, penetrating sound that all the dogs howled as though they had been stung. From the other cells came the murmurs of the monks, as background music for the clatter of my typewriter.

I crept out into the big hall. A score of wax candles were burning in front of the big Buddha—it seemed an ample supply.

"Good Buddha, may I borrow one? *You* don't have to use a typewriter."

Was it sacrilege to steal from Buddha? In any case he did not seem to be angry.

"Good Buddha, are you also in this game? And are you smiling in spite of it? Are you now quite sure that in me you have gained yet another adherent to your great following which makes up such a large part of the world's population?"

As I crept by with the candle it seemed as though the Buddha winked. But what he thought of me, Buddha alone knows.

To-day my scalp will be shaved as smooth as a billiard ball, and I will don the saffron robe. The abbot gave me one more short tutorial.

"To-day, when you become a *koo yien*, you are going to be regarded as a child, and so you will have a young girl to accompany you the whole time and help you to avoid transgressing the monastic rules. And you must not leave the monastery grounds."

"Oh, won't I be able to go out to collect food?" I asked.

"Yes," laughed the monk. "That's an exception from the rule, but even then you won't be alone, for whilst you are still only a few days old there will always be someone to escort you and look after you. This is so that you quickly accustom yourself to all our rules, so that you don't offend the people outside. Do you think that from now on you can live on only one meal a day?"

"Sure," I replied in American. It sounded a little blasphemous, and the abbot must surely have known the word, for he laughed again when the interpreter had translated it.

I was just about to tell him about an elephant hunt, where for three months we only fed in the evenings, because we could walk faster on empty stomachs. But then I remembered that the abbot abhorred killing, and also the elephant is a sacred animal.

"So now I can no longer go on safari?" I said.

"Yes, you can later on, if you really want to. But not while you are wearing the *tchingan*, not while you are clad in the saffron robes. But it is always wrong to kill, so it would be better if you didn't do it. It would also be a good thing if you never drank alcohol. But this is one of the most difficult things to get people to give up," he said and laughed, as though this obstinacy in some way appealed to his sense of humour.

Now, at the eleventh hour I had to ask one more question before my ordination, a question I had long thought about.

"Holy abbot," I said, "I have great sympathy with Buddhism and to-day I can completely hold to the rules which apply to a *koo yien* but I cannot promise that in, say, six months or a year, I will still be thinking along the same lines. I am not familiar with what you call meditation, and my understanding of rebirth is not completely clear. Would it be wrong for me to become a *koo yien* on this basis?"

"No, my friend," replied the abbot. "You can certainly become a *koo yien*; it will be a gain both for you and for us, regardless of what your future may hold. But naturally we hope that you will return to live with us in the monastery on some future occasion. And we hope that when you write your books you will tell your people what it feels like to become a *koo yien*. We are all very grateful to you, because by your efforts you have set an example for others to follow."

The town was in festive mood, with everyone smiling happily. Hundreds of the leading townspeople would be arriving here, led by the mayor, and there would also be many of the abbots from the neighbouring pagodas and monasteries. I was really rather embarrassed at all the fuss.

Once more I stood in my cell and watched as the brilliantly clad people climbed the hill. Men with pleasant, happy faces, chattering women, and children who looked like china dolls. The drums began to play in the big hall—in a few moments I would be ordained. And I intended to do the thing properly.

I washed my hair—it was easier to do this while it was still there. I was so tied to worldly vanity that rather than throw it away I wanted to keep it as a memento. I had just finished doing this when there was a knock on the door. I was ready, so let them all come—or so I thought.

In came a young man in khaki uniform.

"I am from the police. Your visa expired long ago. It is very serious. Please come with me at once to the police station."

CHAPTER XI

Initiation

A visa indeed! As if there had been time to think about anything as worldly as a visa. Were all my efforts going to be wasted by this bit of bureaucracy? And I thought of all the people to whom the festival was giving so much happiness. They certainly must not be disappointed.

"Can't you postpone it for another day?" I asked. "I am just about to become a monk."

For a moment I thought of gagging him and leaving him in the cell until the ceremony was over, but he was big and strong, and he had a sword. Then I had a better idea.

"May I see the order?"

"It is a verbal order."

"Verbal?" I said sceptically. "I wonder if you have not misunderstood the chief of police? I must ask you to be so good as to come with your chief's written order, and I will promise not to leave the monastery to-day."

For a moment the khaki-clad youth hesitated. Then he left.

I knew there was no chance of him getting back before the ceremony began and he would not dare to interrupt it. How could he arrest me once I had become a monk? You can't arrest a monk with impunity. If one commits a crime the monastery has to give permission before he can be arrested.

A little later there was another knock on the door.

Was it really that policeman again? And had he brought reinforcements?

I retreated into the background and gazed anxiously at the door.

There was another knock. At any rate they were being courteous enough to wait until I opened up.

"Come in," I shouted.

Bat Ears stuck his head in and said there was somebody waiting outside for me.

"Is it the police?" I asked. But when he opened the door wider I saw the Loi Kaw friends who were sponsoring my ordination. There was Daw Sao Mya, the old lady with the Rousseau face; she waited outside whilst U Win Myint and U Kyaw Pe came in with a green *loongyi*, which they wished to present to me.

"It is more practical than European clothes, when the time comes for your change into the saffron robe," said U Kyaw.

"Well, yes, that I can well believe. But I should like to be allowed to pay for it."

"You must get accustomed to forgetting that there is anything called money," replied U Kyaw. "And you also know that good deeds carry their own reward," he added with a smile. "So we are not losing anything."

I stopped protesting and changed into the *loongyi*.

"Remember also to put away your wrist-watch and wedding ring whilst you are a *koo yien*," said U Myint, when he saw me putting my European clothes and pocket-book into a chest.

"Can't I walk around with a watch?" I asked in astonishment. "How will I know the time? Is there something vain about a watch? Surely it's a necessity."

"Perhaps the watch itself is all right, but certainly not the gold strap. But it would be quite in order for you to take off the watch and tie it to the monk's belt which you'll wear under the saffron."

A *koo yien* came to say that it was time for me to come. So with my friends alongside I walked slowly and solemnly through the big hall towards the Buddha.

The place was almost completely filled with spectators from Loi Kaw, and through the big door I could see that the courtyard was crowded with jeeps in which the more prominent visitors had arrived.

When they saw me the music rose to a loud crescendo—a kind of flourish, I thought, a little blasphemously. I glanced at the conductor of the orchestra and recognised him. His last engagement had been to play at the theatre show put on by the casino proprietor. On that occasion there was a piano and a trombone in the orchestra, but now he had to make do with drums, cymbals and other percussion instruments, which are considered correct for a solemn occasion such as this.

I had to turn my back on the orchestra and kneel before Buddha with everyone's eyes on the back of my neck.

Loi Kaw's saffron-clad monks sat side by side on a dais near to the Buddha. In front of them stood a row of large basins, which were filled with wax candles, matches, sardines in oil, condensed milk and other articles which had been presented to the monastery in honour of the occasion.

The eldest monk recited some verses in Pali which I had to repeat. Suddenly I became very nervous. I was sure that yesterday I knew all the verses inside out, but now I just could not recognise the words. I thought back to what my Minifon had said and by speaking sufficiently low and indistinctly I managed to get through it all without anyone complaining of mistakes.

Last of all came the most important clauses. These I knew well, so not only could I repeat them aloud, but also with conviction:

> Buddham saranam gachami,
> Dhammam saranam gachami,
> Sangham saranam gachami.

Which means:

> I base myself on Buddha
> I follow his teaching
> I support his monastic order.

The time was approaching when they must shave my head. The town's mayor sat down by my side and, through the interpreter, expressed the gratitude and sympathy of his fellow townsmen. As he took leave of me I almost felt like a prisoner about to be led to the scaffold. But it was still some time before my scalp would come under the knife, for suddenly all the monks and visitors left the monastery hall to partake of a feast in one of the adjacent buildings. Only a couple of my friends and I, the direct objects of the feast, were left behind to starve.

After half an hour they all returned, and the orchestra began to boom away again. I was taken into a side room, where the executioner stood ready with the guillotine—no, sorry, where the local barber was waiting with two pairs of scissors and three razors.

U Kyaw dropped his ring into the basin. This is an old custom, which is performed by the future koo yien's father or foster-father— in my case U Kyaw was foster-father. The barber wetted my hair and then started cutting it, using scissors and razor alternately. I was surprised that he did not ask whether I would like the hair clippers on my neck.

The razor scratched against my scalp as the hair fell. It sounded like a nail against sandpaper, even though the orchestra was still thundering away in Buddha's hall.

I had hired the local street photographer and a wheelwright from the town to operate my cameras. I had previously told them to fire away for all they were worth, in the hope that I might get at least one usable picture.

The street photographer managed fairly well—indeed he ought to have had some knowledge of the job—even though the pictures I had seen in his show-case in the street suggested that this was not very detailed. The wheelwright was not so good. What was the use of my having carefully explained the apparatus beforehand, if he held his thumb in front of the lens the whole time?

Whilst my hair was falling off I should have been thinking that this symbolised the frailty and decay of the body. Thinking too about how to live an exemplary life, so that all the inhabitants of Loi Kaw could respect me, as they had looked forward to doing, so that through my good example they themselves should come to lead a good and moral life. Instead of this I could not help thinking of that blockhead of a wheelwright and his wretched thumb.

In fact I did *try* to be serious, and I was really rather ashamed that I did not succeed. But in my own defence I must say that the good barber, his assistant and my two sponsors from Loi Kaw, were all being a little frivolous.

Suddenly it dawned on me that there was no need to be too pompous about it all, for ceremony itself is not of great significance for Buddhists. The ordination is only a festival, a kind of examination party, to celebrate the fact that I was now being promoted into a higher class.

In the same way—apart from the fire hazard—it was in no way offensive that Maung Maung Hong puffed away at a big cigar whilst holding the cloth into which my hair was falling.

Perhaps it was this simple happy atmosphere that was so attractive. True enough we had our Buddhist monastic Latin, the sacred Pali tongue, but to me it did not inspire the awe of Roman Catholic church Latin. Far more important than the ordination ceremony itself was whether in the coming days I should be able to keep the rules of the monastery.

The orchestra was playing a little less loudly, and soon afterwards a couple of men looked in.

"It's taking longer than usual," they complained.

"It's the beard," answered the barber as the last red tufts fell to the ground.

Tonsured and clean-shaven by the careful barber I was finally led into the hall, and with the orchestra playing forte fortissimo the saffron robe was draped around me; the worldly green *loongyi* fell to the floor behind me and I was led up to the dais.

I had become a *koo yien*.

People touched their foreheads to the ground in front of us. Now this really *was* a solemn occasion—that is, until the twenty-year-old *koo yien*, whom I called Yul Brynner, nudged me in the ribs, winked and whispered:

"O.K!"

This was the only English he knew and perhaps it sounded more emotional in his ears than in mine.

The mayor again thanked me on behalf of the town, but this time he knelt in front of me. Then the interpreter too knelt at my feet and asked if the holy monk would speak to the people.

The holy monk was not prepared for this, but there was so much I would gladly have said to all these people, who, although I was a foreigner, had taken care of me and had been so considerate that I felt I really belonged.

With the interpreter translating I began:

"Burmese friends!

"It is a common human urge to seek a philosophy of life, and so I have not only studied the Christian religion, which prevails in my own country, but have also attempted to study other religions. Some have repulsed me, others attracted me.

"When I came to Buddhism I was struck by its tolerance and logic, its simple and human ethics, and I wanted to learn more. But I live in a distant land, where there are no Buddhists; I had to rely on books. Now that I have come to Burma, I have been interested to see how Buddhism works in practice. But I had never suspected, never dreamt, that I should meet such kindness and helpfulness.

"Monks and townsmen of Loi Kaw, I thank you from the bottom of my heart for helping me to learn more about Buddhism, so that in the coming weeks I can live within your monastery in accordance with its rules.

"My job is to write about what I see and experience, and I could not write a book on Burma without having a close knowledge of Buddhism. It would not have been adequate merely to write about the monks as I have seen them in the streets, and to collect information at third or fourth hand. But whatever my thoughts about and attitude to Buddhism may be in the future, that which has happened to-day will be of great significance to me and also to the people for whom I write.

"You have made great sacrifices to prepare the festival meals which have just been served. Gifts have been made to the monastery. But, above all, I am grateful to you for the interest and friendship you have shown towards me."

After my speech there was a murmur of approval, and then we arranged ourselves for photographs out in the monastery courtyard. It seemed as though all the cameras in the town were clicking away.

There was indeed no doubt that the town was really delighted that a new *koo yien* had been admitted. Several of the townspeople came afterwards to my cell and knelt before me. First came the mayor and then the grannies and the doddering old men, who had to be helped on to their feet again.

I touched my bald pate. I suppose it was all right, if it gave them pleasure. But could I really set an example to these people, who seemed to me to have so many qualities which I myself as a European lacked?

Indeed the more I came to know the Burmese the more it seemed that it was I who should be kneeling in front of these high-thinking people. I myself would only be holding to the ordinary monastic rules for some weeks or months, but these folk had complied so well with Buddhist teaching that it literally illumined their pleasant, friendly faces.

I had just seen myself in the looking-glass—I was quite unrecognisable. The dog I met at the foot of the stairs was just as surprised as me. It usually barked so furiously that I had often feared for my bare legs. When I approached on this occasion it remained quite silent. Once it had recognised my scent, however, and realised who was hiding away in the saffron robe it gave a disconcerted snivel and stuck its tail between its legs.

Outside my cell I met the two little girls. I wanted to give them my comb, for which I had no further use, but at first they were so bashful

Excitement among the marionettes in the house on stilts as a white man sails by in the canal down below

The little koo yien is not, of course, praying, but thinking about Buddha's good deeds both as an ideal and a guide for himself

that they almost ran away. Bat Ears came to my rescue, and when they understood that this was a present they were so pleased that tears came into their eyes.

Several days later I saw that they were still carrying the comb around, and now and then they would take it in turn to comb each other's hair.

Suddenly the khaki-clad police constable appeared—I had completely forgotten him. He touched his head three times on the ground.

"Your holiness must think no more about the visa—not even when you become an ordinary man again."

"There were two rather serious mistakes in your speech to the people," said the abbot the same evening.

"Mistakes?" I replied in astonishment.

"You thanked the people from your heart, because they had helped you."

"Yes, it was so kind of them."

"Quite so, but good deeds carry their own reward. When people do what is right they become better people and come closer to salvation. Therefore you should not thank them."

This, I thought, was in a way parallel with the modern psychological theory that there is an element of egoism in our "good" deeds, and I felt ashamed of my error. But my thoughts were interrupted by the abbot who suddenly gave a hearty laugh. He was staring at my tiny sandals.

"I normally wear size eleven," I said, a little offended.

To the Burmese my feet were enormous, and they had been unable to find a single pair of sandals to fit me.

"You've only got three toes in your sandals," said the abbot.

"Yes, but even that is better than walking barefoot on the sharp gravel in the courtyard, and among the thorny mimosa bushes."

"It was never Buddha's intention that you should become a fakir," he said kindly. "So you must certainly wear your own sandals, even though they are not regulation monk's pattern, but remember to take them off when you go inside and also when you go down to the town to collect food."

"That is welcome news," I said.

"Yes," continued the abbot. "And that, you see, is why you need a companion during the first few days, so that you can be reminded of what is right and what is wrong. In other respects you can live quite a pleasant life. You will receive food and shelter, and you need have no worries, so long as you wear the saffron robe."

"Except to worry about whether the robe is falling off," I interjected, as I struggled to keep the saffron sheet in place.

The abbot laughed. "We all have had that difficulty, but you'll soon learn. It's about time," he added, "that you received a name. As long as you are divine you must not use the name you had when you were a man. So I have decided that you shall be called Samanera Nyanagavesi."

"What does it mean, Holy abbot?"

"You have been a very industrious pupil, and so I have chosen the name which means 'he who tries to learn everything about Buddha'."

The abbot continued. "In addition to the ten commandments which, as I have told you, every *koo yien* must obey, you must also learn to eat properly. I shall now tell you some of the rules which Buddha laid down two thousand five hundred years ago."

And he rattled off a string of orders, some of which I recollected from my earliest childhood.

Sit up properly at the table. (Not so simple, when the table is ten inches high, and you are sitting on the floor.)

Eat tidily and don't play with your food.

With rice take only a quarter portion of meat or curry.

Don't fill your mouth too full.

Don't stick all five fingers into your mouth. (You always eat with your fingers!)

Don't stick your tongue out when the food is entering your mouth.

"This of course is what many women do to protect their lipstick," added the abbot, "so the rule is just as important to-day as it was 2,500 years ago."

Don't chew noisily.

Don't drink noisily.

Don't lick your fingers.

Don't lick your lips.

There was a great clap from the half-moon shaped gong—it was time to say good night to Buddha. There were always fresh flowers on the altar, and Buddha received three meals a day.

"But he doesn't eat them, so why do you do this?" I had asked on my first day.

"Nor can he smell the flowers," was the reply. "Yet you are not worried about us putting them in front of his statue. Just as we like to give him flowers so do we also like to put a good meal in front of him."

We then knelt in front of the altar.

I must admit that I was thinking just as much about the steaming bowl of rice as about Buddha. As a *koo yien* I would only get one meal a day. Buddha just smiled. A little mischievously, perhaps?

CHAPTER XII

The Monastic Life

THE MONASTERY DAY began at five in the morning, with five ear-splitting claps from the big gong. You woke with a start—if you were not already awake—for the din was such that the dogs howled and the little birds almost dropped from the trees.

A moment later we had to say good morning to Buddha in the great hall. There we squatted for quarter of an hour, thinking about his good deeds, and how we could follow his example. As saffron-clad monks we sat in front, and behind us were the schoolchildren in three long rows.

I found it difficult to think about Buddha when my legs ached so badly. You need training to sit like this for fifteen long minutes, and I knew that the schoolchildren too, the little brutes, were also not thinking about Buddha, for they had long ago noticed that I found difficulty in squatting and now they were eagerly waiting for me to fall over.

It would not have been wrong if I had changed my position and had sat on the floor with my legs stretched out. But I refused to give in. I wanted to show that if the others could do it, then so could I.

One morning things really went wrong. I had sat the whole fifteen minutes in the correct position, with my arms clamped against my sides to hold the saffron sheet in place. But several times I had had to shift my weight from one leg to the other, and each time the robe had slipped a little farther down. Doubtless the youngsters behind me had been sitting in breathless expectation, their eyes glued to the spot, instead of thinking about Buddha. I myself did not notice anything, until I had to struggle to my feet again. When I tried to lever myself up, using both arms and my poor cramped legs, I noticed—but too late—that I was treading on the sheet.

The youngsters had a good laugh when I fell over.

"Are you laughing at a holy monk?" I asked, as I tried to regain my composure and dignity.

"You don't look like a holy monk, for a monk is supposed to move about unobtrusively and under control," answered one of the brighter sparks.

And then the remainder laughed so heartily that there was nothing else to do but laugh with them.

But my little friends made up for their disrespect by spending a whole hour instructing me in the difficult art of how to wear the saffron robe correctly.

Two of them stood on their stools at my side, whilst the others grouped themselves around me, and tried hard to teach me how to put on the saffron *tchingan*. Not only in the carefree manner used in the monastery precincts, but also in the formal "mummy style"; that is with the ends and corners fastened at wrist and armpit in such a way that you can scarcely breathe, let alone move your arms, without risk of the whole thing falling off and landing round your ankles.

I have always considered it quite an ordeal to wear evening dress with a stiff shirt—but I am quite convinced that the "mummy style" is infinitely more painful.

The youngsters were delighted when they had finally managed to wrap the *tchingan* round me in the proper way. At that moment, however, the senior monk came in and reproached them for standing on the stools, because this placed them higher than me, and they must never look at a holy man from above.

One day I got permission to accompany the abbot on a visit to one of the neighbouring monasteries.

The tropical sun beat down on my bald pate as I set off close behind my tutor. He also must have felt the heat on *his* shaven head, for throughout the journey he held up his big fan as a shade.

I also had my fan, but could not use it, because I had to keep my arms close to my sides to hold the saffron sheet in place. It had been fastened in all directions, but the material kept slipping farther and farther down. How embarrassing it would be if I lost my monk's robe on the public highway.

We had still a long way to go and I realised that I would never reach the monastery without a serious mishap. Fortunately the abbot noticed my predicament and found that we could pay a visit to a house close by. There I succeeded in adjusting my troublesome dress—but only just in time.

I rather enjoyed being outside the monastery again. I walked with great dignity, as was befitting; did not step out to avoid puddles, but went straight ahead, gazing at the road three yards in front of me, just as I had been taught. Really I ought to have been pleased at the chance of a walk in the countryside, but I still found myself yearning for the peace of my cell, where during the last few weeks I had got through more writing than I normally did in two months.

The abbot of the neighbouring monastery was old and infirm; he lay on the floor surrounded by a forest of medicine bottles. This rather surprised me, but my tutor was obviously used to finding him like this. The old man staggered to his feet to receive my greeting. Whilst the two monastery principals were chatting I had a chance to look around.

It was an old monastery, with a thick layer of dust on the ceiling rafters. Here the Buddha did not have so many fresh flowers as in my own monastery, but on the other hand he was surrounded by a mass of smaller Buddha figurines—plus a giant owl made of papier mâché and gold paper. I wondered what connection this had with Buddhism, but I was later told that it was just a present from the schoolchildren, who had made it themselves.

The schoolroom was in a side wing. Here there were no tables or chairs, and the little pupils lay on the floor, their tongues following the pencils as they wandered back and forward across the slates. They were so engrossed in their work that they did not notice my entry; and not once as I wandered around did they allow themselves to be distracted—but of course I was just another monk and so nothing out of the ordinary.

At one end of the room a monk was teaching arithmetic, at the other end a young *koo yien* was giving instruction in calligraphy. When they came up to show their work the pupils bowed with natural respect before their divine teachers—here at any rate discipline was no problem.

Even on a weekday like this the little girls were as beautifully dressed as they would be for an examination, and the flowers in their hair looked so fresh that I was sure they had been out to pluck them during their break. It was obviously regarded as an honour and a privilege to be allowed to attend school.

As we were leaving, Saddhammofrale asked whether I would not like to sit on the big peacock throne by the side of the Buddha so that the interpreter could take a picture of me.

"You're joking," I replied. "Surely a *koo yien* can't occupy such an elevated position."

"Oh, yes," said the abbot, "you can certainly sit up there. Of course, I myself must go out in the meantime, for, as you know a *koo yien* must not sit higher than an abbot."

And this is how it came about that I was photographed in the handsome golden chair, which was inlaid with brilliantly coloured glass beads —were they real rubies?

It is not blasphemy for a newly appointed *koo yien* to fill such an elevated seat because, according to Buddhist teaching, objects in themselves are of no religious significance. The peacock throne was regarded as a necessity. It would have been quite different if, from my high seat, I had felt myself to be spiritually elevated above the abbot.

On the way home to our own monastery we passed the local retreat for meditation. This consisted of a small temple for communal meditation and a score of little huts for private meditation. Close by there was a short "track," a philosopher's path, where you could walk up and down while thinking.

"When you meditate," the abbot told me, "you should preferably sit with crossed legs and concentrate on your breathing."

This sounded rather difficult. "If non-Buddhists can attain Nirvana," I said, "Buddhists should be able to reach it without meditation."

"Yes, they *can*, but nevertheless meditation is very important. It takes a long time to understand what the word really means, and even longer to learn how to put it into practice."

"Why is meditation so important?"

"That is what is so difficult to make you understand," sighed the abbot. "But you see, it is through meditation that you form some idea of Nirvana; for a few hours you can feel yourself free from an earthly existence."

My more worldly interpreter, in whose Buddhism I had little confidence, wanted to add his own explanation of the problem, and said seriously:

"You have a feeling of paradise, a glimpse of the supernatural, of Nirvana, in the same way as ordinary men feel at the supreme moment of love."

At this moment a jeep stopped alongside us. It was Reza and one of his friends. They bowed to us and asked whether they could drive us back to Uttararama monastery.

It was apparently quite in order for monks to ride in a jeep. We climbed on board and set off to the monastery with our saffron robes flapping around our ears, and at a speed which was not quite proper for holy men, whose duty it is to preserve dignity.

The chauffeur beamed with pride at being allowed to give two monks a lift—perhaps he thought this would bring him a couple of miles nearer to Nirvana. At any rate the trip brought us two nearer to our midday meal, which it would otherwise have been difficult to consume before twelve noon.

We ate the only meal of the day (as usual a portion of rice) in a room attached to the kitchen. The senior monks had to go in first. Then later when I and my contemporaries entered we had to kneel before them. After that we were allowed to sit down at our table.

Before my ordination I had to sit on a bast mat, but after I had become divine I was provided with a red cloth. We sat cross-legged on the floor and ate from a low table. In addition to the dish of boiled rice there were some small bowls full of remarkable trimmings. I had forced myself to try them all—I don't know which tasted the worst, but to me they were all rather unpleasant. So usually I only took the boiled rice, which according to custom I ate with my fingers.

The monks were obviously sorry for me, and offered to prepare special dishes for me, but this I would not allow. I wanted to show them that I too could live in the same way.

For the last few days I had had a remarkable rash over my whole body; it disappeared during the day, but became more irritable every morning—it was particularly bad on my arms and hands. It could scarcely have been caused by too much food, for I only ate a sparrow's ration.

One night I dreamt that both my arms were buried in a big ant-hill. Surely they could not be bed-bugs? During my previous journeys in the tropics I had often been bitten by these vermin, which you cannot avoid; but I had never *seen* a bed-bug, except in a book on zoology.

The planks of my bed were covered only by an old felt carpet; a mattress would have been too great a luxury for an ascetic monk. When I lifted the carpet I saw several small insects scurrying about on the boards and disappearing into the crevices. I took them to be a local kind of cockroach—and cockroaches were nothing to worry about. On the contrary, they would eat up the bed-bugs.

Yul Brynner came in, and as soon as he saw the small cockroaches he started the hunt. The "cockroaches" *were* bed-bugs. They were swarming around between his fingers and I was just about to fetch something to squash them with, when I saw him carefully carrying a captive over to the window and throwing it out on the grass.

And then I remembered: "thou shalt not kill." Nevertheless I asked him whether it would be all right to use petrol or poison. Yul Brynner was so shocked at the thought that he dropped a newly-caught insect.

"But then they would die," he shouted.

"Oh, yes, of course, and naturally we can't have that."

We managed to catch several dozen of the little beasts. Yul Brynner went to work systematically. Plank by plank, he carefully searched every crack and crevice. The catch was handed to me and I carried it to the window and respectfully threw it out. Suddenly I heard a loud wail from my fellow huntsman.

There he stood holding a damaged bed-bug, as distressed as if it had been an injured nestling bird. The animal had hidden itself in a crack in the timber and he had broken two of its legs in trying to fish it out with a splinter of wood. It had also probably suffered some internal damage and now lay in his hand, not knowing whether to live or to pass over into the next incarnation.

For a minute we stood with bated breath, watching what we thought were its death throes. Then suddenly the crisis passed and the animal valiantly crawled away on its remaining legs. We both breathed a sigh of relief.

But now the hunt became even more dramatic, for a moment later a bed-bug slipped into a crevice in the foot of the bed. To reach it Brynner put his shoulder against the bottom bar of the bed; the board gave and the bug crawled farther in. Brynner's shoulder began to tire, but if he released the pressure the crevice would close up and the bed-bug would be crushed. I also had to give a hand, but we still could not reach the bed-bug. So Brynner shouted to the other monks who came running in to help. After a hair-raising chase, which involved the use of a crowbar, we managed to split the bed apart and the bed-bug came out with all its legs intact. It was of secondary importance that the bed had lost two of its legs, and to show goodwill I did not throw the little beast out of the window, but carried it the whole way down the steps and placed it on a bush. It would have been easier with Flit, I thought heretically.

Sometimes we went out in the mornings to collect food—it is not correct to call it begging, for that is absolutely forbidden. We were not allowed to ask for anything specific, but people came to us voluntarily and gave us small gifts.

At first it was difficult for me to adjust myself to this, but after I had seen how the system worked, I could find nothing objectionable. People did not give for our sake, but for their own; indeed it is always gratifying to the conscience to give presents. Most of them gave a bowl of boiled rice, which was worth about a farthing; a few gave larger gifts. This is really no more than the clergy in a Christian church asking the congregation to put a coin in the poor box.

Before I set out on my first collecting trip a boy sat down on the mound outside the monastery and beat a small gong. This could be heard in the town and was a signal that those who wanted to present a handful of rice could set about preparing it.

On this trip I again had proof of how pleased the people were at having a new monk.

I walked rather carefully in my saffron robe modestly holding my arms close against my sides. A little boy from the monastery school showed me the route I was supposed to take.

When collecting you have to walk barefoot—and unfortunately they had just spread new sharp gravel on the road, so I felt like a fakir, but the pain was soon lost in amazement at the amount of food I received. Outside the houses women and children stood in queues with their bowls, and in a few minutes my jar was full of rice; then somebody presented me with a basket, to which the rice was transferred, and the little school-boy asked to be allowed to carry it. A minute or two later the basket was full and then I got more baskets and more little porters. A couple of adults joined the procession and carried a big chip basket slung between them on a pole. Later on they hung it on a bicycle. One of the men knew a little English, and every time I wanted to turn home he persuaded me to go on a little farther.

"You mustn't disappoint all those who are waiting with their gifts," he said.

Small children, and wrinkled old men and women came and knelt before me—some were so old that they had to be helped on to their feet again. My pious life would serve as a model to help them to improve themselves.

I began to understand why I ought not to kill a bed-bug; the fact that the holy monk will not kill even such a small and unpopular animal makes it easier for the ordinary man to respect life as a whole. He may kill both bed-bugs and mosquitoes with D.D.T., but perhaps with a bad conscience, and he would think twice before killing a more highly organised animal. At any rate, wherever the Buddhist philosophy prevails you never see the cruelty to animals which is so common in many other parts of the world.

By the time I got back to the monastery I had a score of boys behind me, all carrying small gifts: a little meat, a little curry, some fish, something that looked like lugworms, and so on. In addition I had collected so much rice that three men and a bicycle could only just manage it.

Now we certainly had enough food for two days, for the monks as well as the schoolchildren and the poor, so to-morrow I would not need to walk barefoot over the sharp gravel.

When I had washed the mud off my feet and had returned to my cell I received a deputation from the village. They asked if I would be so kind as to go collecting again to-morrow, in that part of the town where I had not been to-day, because there were so many who wanted to be allowed to give presents.

The four men knelt on the floor and waited for my reply. How could I say no?

My feet were sore and I was dead tired from the long walk and from lugging the basket. This sort of trip is exhausting when you only get one meal a day.

"Friends, I shall come, but only give small presents, for we now have enough food for ourselves and the poor. But we value your generosity and we will not disappoint you to-morrow."

The four men bowed gratefully, touched their foreheads on the floor, and backed out of the cell.

It is an honour to be thought worthy of walking out with a basket to receive gifts. But I could not help wondering whether I was worthy enough, for during my collecting trip I had been rather conceited about the large amount of rice I had collected. For when I saw the long line of porters following me, I reckoned, in typical European fashion, that it must almost have been a record for the monastery.

In conversation with Saddhammofrale I told him of my qualms.

"It is perhaps because you have these worries that you are worthy. It is such a short time since you were an ordinary man that you may still make mistakes. But, in spite of everything, you know that it is not the quantity you collect that is important, and that a monk who humbly returns with only one small bowl of rice may be better than you."

CHAPTER XIII

Back to Normality

"YOU HAVE been a good pupil, Samanera Nyanagavesi," said the abbot on one of my last days in the monastery, giving me one of his gentle smiles.

I knelt and touched my head on the ground—once would have been enough, but I did it three times, for I especially wanted to express the greatest possible respect. I had grown to like this man. He had such a fine character, was so thoughtful and considerate. When he sat in front of the Buddha his exemplary goodness made him seem divine, yet at the same time his happy smile and gentle laughter made him so human.

"You have learned the fundamentals of Buddhism, and you can continue to improve yourself after you have left me. We Buddhists believe that, whether you follow the teaching of Christ or Buddha, you can be saved, provided you are good and behave correctly."

"This tolerance towards other men's thoughts is one of the things that attracts me, Abbot. I have never been able to agree that according to some Christian teaching, my friends among the African pigmies, among the savages of South America and many others I have known in other parts of the non-Christian world, should strictly speaking all be destined for hell."

"If a man touches a piece of glowing coal he will burn his fingers—whether he is yellow, black or white and irrespective of race or religion. On the contrary we believe that if a man is good, it will go well with him. That is why we are able to respect the beliefs of others."

And the abbot continued seriously: "You will become good, if you respect our five ideals: the good Buddha, his rules for life, his disciples, your parents—and the teachers you have had during your life, for learning is very important for our development. With the help of learning it is easier to distinguish between good and bad."

All of a sudden the abbot stopped and stared at me.

I almost became afraid! I was quite certain that the mosquito I had flicked away with a reflex movement was laid out flat on my bald scalp.

I had broken the first and most important commandment.

"Holy abbot, how can I now atone for my offence?" I asked, nervously.

"That you cannot do," he replied, with a smile. "You know that just as you cannot bring the mosquito back to life, so you cannot undo those things which are already done. But there is no harm in it, if you humbly employ this moment in deciding to do a good deed."

"Holy abbot, I shall shortly become an ordinary mortal. Would it be a good deed if I were to give a big present to the monastery, when I leave?"

"It is not the size of the gift that matters, but the kind thought," he replied, and smiled a little reproachfully at me. "It were better if you visited some other monasteries and temples, and there thought about Buddha's deeds."

"A journey perhaps to the Golden Pagoda in Rangoon and to the temples in Bangkok?" I asked.

"Yes," replied the abbot, "that would be good for you, and also you should extend your tour to Cambodia, for I believe that in the old temples at Angkor Vat, almost overgrown by jungle, you would find something particularly significant."

The sin I had committed by killing the mosquito was forgotten in a moment—even though, according to Buddhism, it had been entered into my life's balance sheet. I was already thinking about new journeys to strange lands and wonderful temples.

I was kept busy during my last few days as a monk, for the invitations flowed in from the leading families of the village, and the abbot certainly had a problem in selecting the few which we could afford to accept. Since a monk may only eat once a day you can't go to many parties.

One day we accepted an invitation from the married couple Mya Twin. The wife was a Christian and taught in a mission school, but the husband was a Buddhist.

We wrapped ourselves up tight in our saffron robes, and with clattering sandals, I set off behind the abbot and one of the other senior monks.

Pedestrians moved aside for us and the cyclists we met on the path rode right out into the grass as we went by. A yellow-brown cur barked at us, but it was probably a Christian hound!

When we reached the Twins' little timber villa we went through an attractive flower garden, up some steps of rough planking and left our sandals outside, before treading on to the room's plaited mat.

At the door the ten-year-old Tun Twin was kneeling with a white cloth to wipe the dust from the road off our feet; after this we entered the spotlessly clean room. I thought of the Old Testament prophets who had their feet washed before sitting down to the fatted calf.

In the Twin home everything had been scrubbed and swept, the table-cloth had been starched and ironed, and the incredible number of bowls with fragrant concoctions was enough to make three hungry monks water at the mouth.

The grand luncheon was laid out on two tables; at one sat the abbot and the old monk; as a *koo yien* I myself was not worthy of sitting at the same table as them, so was shown to the other one.

In addition to ourselves there were some female guests, who sat on the floor near the kitchen. They had come in their best clothes—blouses in pastel shades of blue and lilac, yellow scarves, flowered skirts, flowers behind their ears and in their hair. And I don't think I exaggerate when I say that the layer of powdered bark which covered their faces must have been at least an eighth of an inch thick. To European eyes the powder had been rather slovenly smeared on. But it is distinguished to have such a layer of powder, and it is said to make the skin soft and supple.

A moment later one of the ladies hauled out a colossal cigar. It was as thick as a baby's wrist and smoked like a forest fire. Here it was absolutely in order for women to smoke, and, whilst the men were content with cheroots or ordinary cigars, the women as a rule preferred these monstrous green maroons.

After so many Spartan days in the monastery the smell of this luxurious meal was very tempting. Nevertheless I am so much the photographer that pictures were more important than food, and so I asked the abbot if he would object to my taking some photographs.

"My friend," he replied, in a matter-of-fact voice. "It is half past eleven and we cannot eat after twelve. If you begin to take photographs now we won't taste the good food at all. It would be better to wait until afterwards."

The food tasted splendid, but as a monk I could only allow myself a tiny bit of meat with each dish of rice. Nevertheless this was a chance to make good some of the two or three pounds' weight I had lost in the monastery. But I was much handicapped because once more I was losing my saffron robe. I only dared to reach out for the nearest dishes and I ate as carefully as possible; in spite of this the sheet slipped farther and farther down. I felt disaster approaching and finally I could not move at all and had to swallow the food with my eyes. Luckily my dear abbot noticed my dilemma and, asking the women to retreat for a moment to the kitchen, helped me so that I could start in again.

Mrs. Twin went to and fro with the scented dishes which she passed to Mr. Twin, who served us, kneeling.

I had no watch with me, but the abbot obviously had an internal clock, and I knew for certain that when he stopped eating it must be noon.

After the meal we were served with cigars and I started taking pictures. The whole family wanted to be photographed. They also asked me to take photographs of the little house-altar, where, to celebrate the occasion, the statue of Buddha was surrounded by a particularly large number of fresh flowers; in addition there was a big basketful of oranges, bananas, coconuts and other fruits.

The family albums were brought out. Amongst other things they contained many pictures of Mrs. Twin at the Christian mission school. She was evidently both a Christian and a Buddhist at the same time—and why not? If you can ignore the less important ones, the basic ideas of the two religions are not really so very different.

As a parting present they gave me a gilded cardboard owl to take home to my children, and a giant cigar for my wife. I am sure that Inge will forgive me for smoking it one evening in my cell, when the sacred mosquitoes were particularly annoying.

When we got back to the monastery I had to kneel three times in front of the abbot and repeat, "May I have permission to become an ordinary man again?" After yet another exhortation to remember to do good, I was allowed to take off my saffron robe.

My European clothes hung loosely about me, and I had to tighten the belt by several holes before I could leave my cell as a man and return to the abbot to thank him for the period I had spent as a monk.

Whilst I knelt before him, he said, "Although you are now an ordinary

A traditional Thai dance, nowadays mainly performed for tourists in Bangkok. The
motif is the victory of good over evil

Above: Siamese dancers. Their dance is completely stylised. *Below left:* Khmer dancers; even in stone they are more natural and life-like. *Below right:* Spectators watching the last act

man again, and need not keep the tenets of Buddhism so seriously, I would nevertheless hope that you will continue to think about Buddha." Saddhammofrale also told me that the time I had spent in the monastery would appear on the credit side when the final balance sheet of my life was drawn up. I truly believed that whoever the accountant might be, the abbot was correct in his assertion.

I walked down from the monastery to Loi Kaw to say good-bye to my friends, and U Saw Hlang accompanied me. When he saw me jump aside to avoid treading on a crowd of ants, he said, with a friendly smile:

"Do you know, I believe you really have acquired several good habits in the monastery."

Everyday life in Loi Kaw went on just as it had before I entered the monastery. Now, nobody knelt to me, but they all gave me a friendly smile. Many came to thank me because my having been a *koo yien* in their monastery had made it easier for them and their children to follow Buddha's good rules for living.

I also met the local Christian missionary.

"I hear you have been a monk in the monastery," he said.

"Yes, that's right," I replied. "What do you say to that?"

"I would be a poor man indeed, and very intolerant if I attacked Buddhism. My Christian mission exists almost exclusively on money provided by Buddhists, who do indeed support anyone who honestly tries to improve himself."

Even my good friend Reza commended me for my time as a monk, in spite of the fact that he himself was a Moslem.

"You ought to know how much you have pleased the village," he said, "it has really made an impression on them. It has made them both better and happier—that is, except for Ihuhu and myself."

"Why are you not pleased about it?" I asked, in astonishment.

"Well, Ihuhu's spirit sales have dropped to a half, and my little cinema is also an entertainment which people are avoiding for the time being. In addition the monks now think that I too should become a monk!" Reza replied, with a smile and a sigh.

"My condolences, my friend," I replied. "But I hope that your success with the coffee bushes will outbalance the loss on your cinema."

"And what if I did let myself be persuaded to become a monk?"

"There would be nothing wrong in that, and you would lose several pounds into the bargain," I laughed.

Reza laughed too.

"Now come inside," he said, "my cook is preparing a gala farewell meal, so that you can recover two or three of the pounds you yourself have lost. Rumour has it that the next aircraft will not arrive for a week, so you have plenty of time to eat."

CHAPTER XIV

Bangkok

FROM LOI KAW I flew back to Rangoon. In the far distance I could see the magnificent Shwe Dagon Pagoda, pointing up to heaven as a reminder to the tiny mortals at its base of the good example set by Buddha.

"Do not visit Shwe Dagon until you have completed your trip to the East," the abbot had said to me in Loi Kaw before I left.

But it is difficult to wait, and for a moment I thought of going straight there. Then I pulled myself together and booked a seat on the next flight to Bangkok.

I regard Bangkok as one of the cities of my youth. It was here, as a sixteen-year-old, that I had my first real taste of travel. I had worked my passage out as a cabin boy on one of the ships of the Danish East Asiatic Company, and during two relatively long stays had gathered material for my first book. Since then I have been in Bangkok several times, but the city still holds the same magic for me.

Up in the aircraft I was keeping an eye out for the first glimpse of Thailand's capital city. The machine began to lose height. The sun's rays were reflected from the flooded paddy-fields, and sparkled brightly on the light cloud cover. It seemed as though they were sending a Morse code signal from land to bid me welcome.

The plane circled for a while over Bangkok, and I recognised the royal palace among all the pagodas which rose towards us.

When I first travelled to Bangkok I brushed the shoes of the infant King of Thailand, Ananda Mathidol, and laughed when his brother, Bhumibol, the present King, handcuffed one of the cabin stewardesses and then pretended that he had lost the key overboard.

Some years later Ananda Mathidol was found dead with a smoking revolver by his side. After this the brother with the charming wife, Sirikit, came to the throne. I am sure that he has now become more serious-minded, although he was quite recently a jazz pianist in New York. In a way he is a sort of colleague of mine, for he has also been a monk, and has walked barefoot through the streets of Bangkok, carrying a bowl to collect his own daily meal. He must find it rather remarkable that people would then have knelt to him with even more reverence than they do now that he is king.

In the airport I once more met the cheerful smiles for which the country is renowned. There was a traffic jam on the way into the city centre, but no one was angry; they just treated it as a joke. They behave in the same way if they break one of the water pots they carry on their heads, or if they have a minor traffic accident. At first this laughing at adversity sounds rather silly to a European. But think how sensible it must be if you can always laugh instead of cursing or swearing.

As always on arrival in Bangkok I immediately took a trip around the city to absorb the atmosphere and to recall the excitement of my first visit. In Denmark I prefer to enjoy the woods and the beautiful country-side on horseback, but I think that Bangkok is best seen from a tram, and it only costs two ticals—about sixpence.

Bangkok's trams have little in common with those of some European cities—in Copenhagen we call them "sacred cows." The Bangkok trams are gay, open cars which glide away gently under the waving palm trees, whilst a pleasant breeze from the Menam River blows in over the ever-smiling passengers. It is almost like being on board a pleasure steamer. There is an atmosphere and solidarity with which the commuters on Copenhagen's trams could never compete. (The only thing Bangkok's trams have in common with those of Copenhagen is that they too were started by a Dane; his name was Aage Westenholz.)

The tram-driver kicks the warning bell with his bare foot. We're off

Enjoy the East's most exciting city for sixpence.

It was evening. Bare-footed girls collected around the communal water-taps in the streets, and the old petrol-cans, carried on yokes over their shoulders, sounded like gongs as they clanked against each other. The roadway was quite flooded with the splashing water and the girls laughed the whole time, their brown cheeks bursting with smiles.

The tram started off; the conductor had difficulty in keeping the white monkey-skin cushions in place in the 1st class section. For a moment the women's laughter was drowned by the clang of the warning bell which seemed to be in tune with the jingling *hti* of the pagodas.

After a few minutes the tropical night shrouded the palm trees in its veil. From every tree and bush came a symphony of cicada songs; the klip-klop of the little girls' sandals on the asphalt blended in with the concert, and the bare feet of the rickshaw coolies smacked against the road, still hot from the sun.

The brightly coloured and more modern cycle-rickshaws were busy now, transporting the sailors from the harbour to the city's nightspots.

The muddy River Menam flowed slowly through the pulsating town, and past the giant pagoda which, like Gulliver in Lilliput, towered high above houses, huts and temples—pointing as though to the moon.

Behind their bamboo walls and curtains Siamese families were lighting their carbide lamps and sitting around chewing betel. The men were playing cards and the women were embroidering their fine silken fabrics. Cockroaches would be swarming in the darker corners. In the king's stable the sacred white elephants were being given their last portion of sugar-cane for the day.

As we approached the city the tram seemed to become less bustling, as though it felt rather out of place in this modern setting. We were overtaken by growling three-wheeler motor-rickshaws and silent purring limousines. Suddenly the passengers became strangers to each other, their faces vacant, and the merry chatter stopped, as though stifled by the cacophony of the big city. The neon advertisements showered us with coloured light.

Soon the modern shops and luxury buildings were replaced once more by teak huts and palm trees. The neon signs were left behind and in the light from the lamps we could see the tropical colours of the bougainvillæa flowers, which in certain places almost smothered the houses.

We put on speed again. The bell clanged repeatedly and the passengers started to chatter once more. We had regained our humour.

We passed gardens, canals, paddy-fields and a planter's bungalow that I had once visited; I particularly remember the nimble little geckos which ran about actively on the ceiling. During the afternoon they sat and stared out into space with lethargic glassy eyes. But at twilight they came to life again, and spent their time running up and down the walls and across the ceiling, hunting for mosquitoes and other insects.

The geckos also enjoyed their love-making up under the ceiling, and it nearly always ended with the entwined pair crashing to the floor —the only time in their lives when they forgot to hold on tight. On one occasion a courting couple fell into the planter's whisky. The houseboy immediately rushed forward to help. The white man grunted, but now and again he didn't really grudge his pets a drink. For a moment the geckos lay unconscious. Then they bustled off up the wall again, apparently unaffected by the strong liquor, and started to hunt for insects as though nothing had happened.

We had reached the terminus in Tanon Tuk, the quarter with the gay night life. An open car drove by with a couple of blond Scandinavian sailors and two coffee-coloured Siamese girls, who were singing "To-night the ship will sail"—in faultless Danish. They were ladies of pleasure from that part of the harbour where the Scandinavian boats dock—not ordinary prostitutes, but the most faithful girl-friends a sailor could wish for. Once they have found a man they will stick to him for as long as his ship remains in Bangkok. And they will fight tooth and nail if an outsider tries to steal him.

There is a very strict code of ethics amongst these girls (many of whom speak Scandinavian), a code which must be observed. It is, of course, unthinkable that they should try to steal men from each other, but occasionally a girl from outside the ring will attempt this, and then she is really in for trouble. She runs the risk of being literally flayed. Very few of these free-lances are able to hold their own at Old Charlie's, the Mosquito Bar or one of the other nightspots frequented by the Scandinavians, where both the owners and the Siamese waiters also speak Scandinavian.

The girls who flit from one man to another are known as butterflies. One of the best-known is the Pirate Queen, who has achieved quite a prominent position as a free-lance, by reason of her great beauty and of certain rare, but hidden qualities.

I suppose the Pirate Queen earns quite a lot more than the regular girls. She is one of the few who are tolerated; mainly, I think, because she is an expert in ju-jutsu. Nevertheless she is despised as a dishonest prostitute, and a sailor who has once had anything to do with her is marked for life and will have a poor chance of finding himself a faithful girl-friend.

The time comes, of course, when the last shore pass has been called in, and Old Charlie's and New Heaven are due for a few days of peace in which to clear out all the empty Carlsberg bottles. Next morning there are touching scenes on the quayside as the ship pulls out. There you will see the angels from Old Charlie's and New Heaven, most of them with tears in their eyes, but some trying to wear a brave little smile. But you won't see the Pirate Queen among them.

"Good-bye, darling," says one of the girls in Danish.

"Don't be a butterfly when you get to Singapore," shouts another.

Back on board the ship's cook finds several pretexts for going over to the railing. The sailors busy themselves with their work and many have a lump in their throats. The young ordinary seaman who has just returned to the ship at the last moment, has been walking around for days contemplating desertion. He stops in the middle of his work and gazes down forlorn at a little dark girl with flowers in her hair and tears in her eyes.

"*Au revoir*," and the girl waves good-bye. In a week's time a new Scandinavian ship will arrive, on which she has another steady friend, but the young seaman knows that when his ship docks again at Bangkok in six months' time his little yellow-brown girl will be waiting on the quay to greet him. He decides never to sail on another route.

To-day the liner's departing siren sounds more jarring than usual and it drowns the girls' farewell cries and sobs.

"Get on with your job," the chief officer shouts to the young sailor. "You'll soon be home to the beech trees of Denmark." But just at the moment the young man prefers palm trees.

The last cable is slipped and slowly hauled on board. The ship stands off in the muddy waters of the Menam and begins the long journey back to the north, but a part of each sailor's heart remains behind in Bangkok.

CHAPTER XV

Angkor Vat

THE TRANSITION from my secluded monastic life in the Burmese monastery to the pullulating life of Thailand's capital city was almost too violent, but a couple of days later when I arrived in Cambodia to see the Angkor ruins I again found solitude.

The myths surrounding Angkor are fascinating and colourful. Eight hundred years before the birth of Christ there lived a prosperous young Indian called Kaudinya. One day he dreamt that he would find a bow, and that after this he would travel to the East. When he awoke he found a bow and also a quiver outside his bedroom. He took this as a sign that the dream had a meaning, and therefore decided to travel.

His ship crossed the Gulf of Bengal, sailed south of the Malayan Peninsula and over the South China Sea to the coasts of Indo-China, where he found his dream fulfilled. Here reigned the Serpent King, whose daughter Willow Leaf set out in her war canoe to attack Kaudinya.

Princess Willow Leaf was the loveliest woman Kaudinya had ever seen, and her beauty was not hidden by even so much as a fig-leaf.

To protect himself, Kaudinya used his magic bow to shoot an arrow through her boat, and Princess Willow Leaf thereupon decided that she would have to conquer him in another way. The meeting, which had started so violently, ended with love and marriage.

They had no quarrels after the first, but lived happily, established a powerful state and became the ancestors of the Khmers, the founders of Angkor. Their female descendants were said to be the most beautiful women in the world.

The serpent, the naga, became the benevolent water-god of the Khmer state, its mother and protector. Even to-day at Angkor you can see numerous representations of the naga. As a rule the snake's body forms

136

a balustrade along the roads bordering the lakes and canals. At the beginning of each road the naga's head with expanded hood is raised to form a kind of portal. The snake symbol is derived from Indian mythology, which provided so many of the cultural accessories of the Khmers.

In his book, *A Short History of Cambodia*, Martin F. Herz tells of another colourful incident from the story of Cambodia. It concerns King Sihanu who was particularly fond of a special kind of sweet lettuce, which only one man in Cambodia knew how to grow. The king decided that he himself would have all the salad that this man could raise. So he constructed a royal salad garden and installed the gardener, whose name was T-Chay, in the honourable office of royal purveyor.

When T-Chay complained that thieves occasionally stole some of the tasty salad, the king gave him a spear and promoted him to the rank of general, so that he was now also the senior guardian of the royal salad garden.

One night, so the legend says, the king had an irresistible desire for some of the fresh, sweet salad—or perhaps he was afraid that thieves had entered the garden. He left his palace accompanied by two female bodyguards.

The night was dark and when T-Chay saw a man approaching he lifted his spear, took aim, and with a powerful thrust pierced the body of his king, who fell dead on the spot.

There was great sorrow in the Palace of Angkor Thom, and soon after the royal council assembled to decide who should succeed the monarch.

They found that there was nobody except T-Chay, who measured up to the old king in virtue and shrewdness. So they decided to set the protector of the royal salad garden on the throne. That is how T-Chay became King of the Khmer State. He married the daughter of the late King Sihanu and founded a new dynasty.

A third story is told about the origin of Angkor Vat, the chief temple. The god Indra took a fancy to a handsome and righteous prince and carried him off to the sacred mountain of Meru, where he had a palace of gold and precious stones. Not long afterwards the beautiful palace dancing-girls, whose job it was to entertain and amuse the prince, complained about his worldly smell, and asked whether he could not be flown back to earth again. The young prince found it difficult to tear himself away from the lovely nymphs and the great luxury, so begged to be allowed to stay. To console him, Indra built Angkor Vat as an earthly annexe to the heavenly palace.

Angkor Vat was coated with gold and glistened with precious stones, and even to this day its bas-reliefs bear witness to the fact that for the prince's enjoyment it was peopled with an army of beautiful earthly dancing-girls, whose noses were less sensitive!

The Khmer kingdom flourished for nearly four hundred years, until in the 14th century it was overthrown by the Siamese; shortly afterwards Angkor was abandoned. At its zenith, however, the country had reached such a high degree of culture that its unique buildings may be compared with the royal palaces and temples of Ancient Egypt. Even to-day one is awe-struck by the architects and civilisation that created Angkor; it seems very unjust that it is not reckoned among the wonders of the world.

In the course of the succeeding centuries the jungle spread in over Angkor. Now only the temples remain, because the ordinary houses were built of wood. But the sanctuaries for the many gods and for the kings, who like some of their Egyptian counterparts were regarded as divine, were built with an eye to posterity. The country is very fertile and the lakes so generous that the fish can be caught by hand. These factors, in combination with their hordes of slaves, gave the Khmers an enormous surplus of labour, making it possible to create these gigantic temples, which cover an area of over seventy-five square miles.

The religion of the old Khmer kingdom came from India. They worshipped Brahma, Vishnu and Shiva and hundreds of lesser gods and spirits—as well as the kings already mentioned. Buddhism arrived later, and the artists and craftsmen had plenty of legends to choose from when seeking motifs for the decoration of the temples.

Many fantastic theories have been put forward to explain why this powerful and cultured city was abandoned. One suggests that a plague killed off all the inhabitants, another that fear of their enemies shattered the population's morale. A third theory suggests that the land became completely exhausted and its people so incapable of work that they were literally starved out. However, the following seems the more probable theory. When the power of the Khmer kings had been broken by Siam, they lost the concentration, power and ability to organise which was so essential if a large population were to live in such a relatively restricted space. As the people only had wooden huts with roofs of leaves or straw, it needed little to drive them away from the town and out into the more fertile areas of open country. The jungle then formed a carpet over the town and Angkor was forgotten.

Then a hundred years ago, the French naturalist Henri Mouhot travelled up the River Tonle Sap and through the jungle area of Cambodia's trackless interior. For several weeks he sailed up the river which was bordered with such dense virgin forest that he could only land by hacking his way in. He had plenty of time to ponder on the stories and rumours about a mysterious jungle town, built of stone, which was supposed to exist somewhere in these parts. In several places he went ashore and hacked a path through the meshwork of lianas, but without finding the slightest trace of ruins. Then one day he saw something that took his breath away: from the top of a high knoll, which looked like a gigantic termite nest, a head ten feet high stared down at him through the branches. Henri Mouhot had found the entrance to one of Angkor's enormous complexes of ruins.

Since then French investigators have worked persistently to free the ruins from the all-embracing roof of jungle. However, in spite of a hundred years of continuous effort in this field, there are still temples which are completely overgrown, and probably many buildings yet to be found.

It is often said that after severe illness or a very dangerous experience one's mind is particularly open to new impressions. Perhaps this is why I was especially receptive for the experience of Angkor, because fate played me an extremely violent and heavy-handed trick, when I was on my way to Cambodia.

It began when we could see some menacing thunder clouds straight ahead of our aircraft. The pilot tried to increase the speed in an attempt to rise above them. This was unsuccessful and we were soon inside a thermal, which was so powerful that the aircraft flapped its wings like an injured duck. It twisted and turned as though we were in a giant harmonica which was playing a twist tune.

The storm became worse and worse, and soon we scarcely knew which way up we were flying; at one moment we spun around like a leaf in a gale.

Then suddenly we realised all too clearly what was beneath us. We had entered an air pocket, free of clouds, which extended down to the ground. Instantly we became weightless. We hung loose in our braces; indeed there was one moment when it felt as though we were bearing the whole weight of the machine. Whilst the earth came rushing towards us I felt like Gagarin or Shepherd in their rockets.

The fall only lasted for about half a minute or less, but the seconds seemed like hours. I cast a terrified look at the steward who had fastened himself into the empty seat next to me, and then I knew indeed that there was cause for fear. Although he must have been quite accustomed to flying, he was grasping the arms of the seat, and was so terrified that his knuckles appeared white through the brown skin.

When we had reached the bottom of the air pocket there was a violent crash, as though we had hit the metal deck of an aircraft-carrier; this was followed by the unpleasant sound of tearing metal. I was propelled forwards with my head pressed down between my knees.

With a great effort I righted myself and then saw the entire cargo of boxes and other baggage sailing along the centre gangway and gliding straight towards the cockpit. The dividing wall to the baggage room had burst.

I felt something cold and wet on my head and for a moment I was certain that there must be a hole in the aircraft and that the rain was pouring in. Then I noticed the remains of a soda-water siphon which had flown out of the pantry and broken against the steward's head. He was bleeding and unconscious and I was just about to go to his help when I myself hit the ceiling; the machine again had its nose pointing towards the paddy-fields, which were now dangerously close beneath us.

"Come quickly," screamed a passenger in front of me and tried in vain to attract my attention by pulling my crew-cut. Then he rushed out into the gangway and down towards the cockpit, starting to shove the boxes towards the rear of the aircraft, and at the same time shouting to the passengers that they should unfasten their belts and crawl to the rear.

Those who were not fast enough got a box in the back. But the plane regained its balance and began to climb again.

In the meantime the steward had regained consciousness and was wiping away the blood. My teeth chattered.

"Sorry, sir," said the man who had laid hands on me. "I was a bit rough when I called to you, but I am a pilot and when the aircraft lost its trim I knew that it was very urgent."

Then he sat down again and opened a newspaper.

I was very impressed, until I noticed that he was holding the paper upside down.

"I think I would prefer to walk back," I muttered to him as we crawled out of the plane at Sem Riep.

"Oh, don't worry," he replied, "it may be months before we get that sort of weather again."

The modern visitor to Angkor is quite unprepared for the surprise he invariably gets, even though he has previously read about it and already seen pictures of the ruins.

From Sem Riep Hotel I drove in a cycle-rickshaw for three or four miles along a half-overgrown jungle road. There was almost no traffic. There were no signposts, no crowds of importunate dragomans or other guides and none of the sightseers you find at the big tourist attractions elsewhere in the world. The few who do come seem infinitesimal in the enormous area occupied by Angkor.

Suddenly the road opened up and straight ahead lay a gigantic moat. Behind it reared the three towers of Angkor Vat's principal temple. They looked like unripe pineapples or lotus buds. A long avenue of stones led from the moat to the temple.

The only living objects I saw were a couple of grazing goats and two monks in saffron robes. But I could well imagine the variegated life which flourished here almost a thousand years ago.

Versailles is only a toy castle compared with the giant buildings of Angkor Vat. The picturesque life at the court of the Roi Soleil must have been a mere shadow of the pageantry enacted when the divine kings of the Khmers set out from the palace, with a retinue of bodyguards and war elephants, and hundreds of dancing girls.

The experts are still in doubt about the exact way in which the temple buildings at Angkor Vat were used; many consider that they originally constituted a mausoleum for King Suryavarman II. But if the history of the place is still obscure, its art is at any rate much in evidence. The splendid bas-reliefs tell us much about daily life, religion and superstition in the remote kingdom of the Khmers.

At one place the reliefs show a boat with a hunting party; one of the men has fallen into the water and is being devoured by an enormous crocodile. At another place the Khmer warriors are fighting with demons that looked like giant apes, smashing them to pieces in a sort of berserk fury. Time and again you come across the wonderful, evocative dancing girls.

The tropical heat and humidity have long ago destroyed the Khmer inscriptions on papyrus and wood. Fortunately, however, the Mongol Chinese Emperor Timur Khan sent Chou Ta-kuan on a mission to Angkor, and from him we can glean something of life in the Khmer kingdom 650 years ago. In his extensive report to Timur Khan, Chou Ta-kuan has done for Cambodia what Marco Polo and William of Rubruck did for China and Mongolia.

Chou Ta-kuan speaks of the splendour and magnificence of Angkor, and we can in part check the accuracy of his detailed report by looking closely at the grey moss-covered stone colossi which remain.

When Chou Ta-kuan undertook his journey Angkor was a brilliant city, where roofs of gold shone in the sun. Even the window-frames were of gold, and on lesser buildings the towers and roofs were of copper. Chou Ta-kuan also writes about the royal procession. The king was preceded by hundreds of dancing girls and other servants, all supported by the palace funds. After them came wagons drawn by goats or horses, with golden harness. The many parasols were also decorated with gold and had golden handles. Then followed the king himself, standing on an elephant so that everyone could see him. He was dressed in armour, with golden jewellery and pearls around his neck, ankles and wrists in such quantity that they almost weighed him down. The king was barefoot, but the soles of his feet and the palms of his hands were painted red, and he held a golden sword. The tusks of the elephants were gilded. Alongside ran the king's female bodyguards armed with spears and shields, and outside them again there were more guards, mounted on horses and elephants.

Chou Ta-kuan also writes of the monks, the king's counsellors, who lived almost like the monks of to-day, of the animal life and of the highly developed agriculture which yielded three or four crops a year.

Chou Ta-kuan was particularly struck by the everyday life of the Khmers—and especially horrified by their morals. Homosexuality was rife, and the women extremely sensuous. One day he heard a woman say that her husband had been away for ten days and this really was too much, for after all, she was a living woman.

In one part of his report Chou Ta-kuan writes of the country's customs, and amongst others of the one known as *chen-t'an*. When the rich girls were between seven and nine years old—the poor ones had to be a couple of years older—a Buddhist priest was given the job of deflowering them. A family with a daughter who was considered ready for *chen-t'an* was sent a candle with a mark on it. When the candle had burned down as far as the mark the time for *chen-t'an* had arrived. Before this the girl's parents had themselves chosen a priest for the job, and they now gave him presents of wine, rice, clothing, areca nuts or silver figurines. There was a big party to which the neighbours were invited, and they built a brilliantly coloured silken hut for the girl.

Chou Ta-kuan was not quite clear about what happened from the time when the monk went in to the little girl until his departure the following morning. Some say that the monk removed the maidenhead by hand, others that he actually copulated with her.

"A Chinaman cannot be present on such occasions, so the exact truth is not known," concludes Chou Ta-kuan.

Angkor consists of thirty extensive complexes. Of these the largest is Angkor Vat, which covers an area of not less than 490 acres. It was built by Suryavarman II (1112-1182). It gives the impression of being even larger than it really is, because the towers are reflected in the Tonle Sap and in the many moats. This gives an effect which has been used in later periods, and indeed even to-day—one has only to think of the Taj Mahal and of the new U.S. Embassy in Tokyo. But at Angkor Vat the reflections in the water are broken by pink lotus flowers.

From the inscriptions one can read that Angkor once had a population of 12,640 people, and that more than 66,000 persons living in the neighbouring area had the job of producing supplies.

The 350-yard-long avenue from the outermost moat up to the main temple is flanked by a balustrade which represents the water god, the naga snake. It is supported by massive stone blocks, and where the balustrade was interrupted for a side avenue leading to the small "library buildings," the snakes raise their heads with expanded hoods.

One of the greatest of Angkor Vat's investigators, Henri Marchal, says that the architectural composition of Angkor Vat is the same as that of the buildings in Classical times, and that the harmony of the proportions has never been excelled. It is, for example, well known that to see a building properly you have to stand at a distance equal to twice its longest dimension. Angkor Vat is 180 metres in breadth, and the avenue from the entrance gate where you first see the temple measures exactly 360 metres.

One characteristic feature of Angkor is the number of tall stone columns found in many of the temples. The explanation for their presence is that while on a visit to Java, Jayarvarman II, one of the kings of Angkor, was inspired to proclaim himself as a reincarnation of Vishnu, the chief god of the Hindus. He therefore took as his symbol the lingam, the gigantic stone phallus which now stands in the central hall of Angkor Vat, the temple which represented the holy mountain of Meru. A whole series of mountain temples were built in the Angkor Vat area, each with the same symbol. The succeeding kings retained the custom and built Meru temples in honour of the lingam. This kind of phallic cult is still found in Java, but it disappeared at Angkor with the advent of Buddhism.

The Angkor ruins bear witness to a peculiar form of religious intolerance, for in one of the transition periods when Hinduism again became popular for a short time a few of the Buddha statues were changed into phallic symbols. Apart from this, however, the old Khmers showed considerable tolerance, and statues of Buddha stand freely side by side with the Hindu gods.

It is well known that there are two opposed Hindu sects, the Shiva and the Vishnu worshippers. In India each sect has its own edition of the god Harihara. But in the Angkor ruins the rivals have reached a solution recalling the judgment of Solomon. Here a statue of Harihara is divided equally through the middle, with a distinct line running down from the hair over the face and body. One half shows the god according to the Shiva interpretation and the other shows the coiffure and clothing preferred by the followers of Vishnu.

Many of the other buildings and rooms at Angkor Vat have been called libraries, but a great number of them must certainly have been schools and workshops for the army of artists who worked on the statues and enormous reliefs (the big wall frieze extending the whole way round the outside of the temple, which is filled with human figures in natural size, is almost quarter of a mile long).

These reliefs are not only of unsurpassed artistic quality, but also express an astonishing and refreshing humanity, and a certain amount of humour. Although the same motifs are repeated hundreds or thousands of times, they do not appear as stereotyped forms and masks. Every single figure glows with life, and the faces are highly individual. One clearly notices the artist's joy in creation—and his own warm laughter. One can imagine him walking about, just waiting for this or that person to

The Khmer buildings show thousands of reliefs depicting the most beautiful women.
Until a few decades ago this wonderful architecture was hidden by the jungle

Above: I had intended that the living elephant should enliven my picture, but it is obvious that against the Khmers' wonderful frieze it appears as though stuffed.
Below: It is some hundreds of years since the Khmers' streets were last weeded

come along and discover that his own face had been used as a model to recreate the religious stories portrayed in stone.

Among these reliefs there is one motif which shows how the evil spirits and the good gods held a meeting to discover whether they could not co-operate to produce the elixir of life which exists at the bottom of the milky sea that surrounds Mount Mandara. A water-god—naturally in the form of a snake—coiled himself round the mountain like a string round a child's top. This is the form which the mountain most resembles when the gods and the demons pull alternately at each end of the snake and thus churn up the sea's milk. Just as the mountain is about to break apart under this unusual treatment, Vishnu changes himself into an enormous tortoise and carries its whole weight on his own broad carapace. The churning continues, whilst remarkable creatures issue forth from the milky sea, amongst them the woman whom Vishnu later marries. But Vishnu has other things to think about than his new wife, for he actually succeeds in finding the elixir of life at the sea bottom. Just as it emerges the treacherous demons try to steal it, but the good Vishnu triumphs over them and returns to the sacred Meru mountain with the elixir of immortality.

The pictures also show how the ten-headed and many-armed demon Ravana abducted Sitra, the wife of the good god Rama, and how Rama won her back in a battle, in which he was helped by an army of monkeys, who used whole trees as clubs to smash the demons.

The reliefs are all very realistic; war is shown in all its horror, without heroic glory. Some of the most dramatic scenes show a naval battle, where the soldiers are pierced by arrows and spears, and in the heat of battle one oarsman falls overboard and is swallowed by a crocodile.

This series of pictures, more than eight hundred years old, also shows the daily life of the Khmers. Here we can see how they built straw-thatched wooden huts, how they fished in the Tonle Sap and grew their rice. On the whole their life was not so very different from that of the present-day Cambodians in the villages nearby.

From the inscriptions we can even read how one of the Buddhist Khmer kings was seized with the desire to do good. Some eight hundred years ago he produced a welfare state, with inns for travellers and hospitals staffed with doctors and nurses, which were collectively ten times as numerous as anything the colonists and Christian missionaries managed to give the country during the long French occupation.

The social welfare work also included the distribution of countless thousands of tons of rice and other victuals, as well as medicines to improve the health conditions in eight hundred villages. These were mainly distributed by the doctors and nurses in the hospitals.

In comparison we can note that when the western civilised world appeared here as a colonial power, there were only two qualified doctors in the whole country. So if Cambodia is now an under-developed country, there is every indication that it has become so since the time of the Khmer kings.

The irrigation system of the Khmers was so finely constructed that even to-day it cannot be improved. Seeing this one is automatically reminded of the Incas, South America's unsurpassed irrigation experts, whose irrigation canals are still in use to-day.

Like the Khmers the Incas were also exceptionally fine builders. They moved stone blocks each weighing several tons without the use of machinery, and both peoples fitted the heavy stone blocks so accurately to each other that they had no need of cement. The Incas had no knowledge of such a binding material, whereas the Khmers produced a very strong vegetable glue which they used in a few cases.

The Incas were, of course, brilliant astronomers. They had a solar year of 365 days and at their stone observatory at Macchu Picchu we again find the astronomical angle of $22\frac{1}{2}°$. On the other hand we know little about the Khmers' understanding of astronomy, and it is possible that it did not have such practical importance in their agriculture as it had for the Incas; nevertheless the Khmers knew enough to orientate their temples exactly east to west.

The Khmers covered their palace roofs with gold, the Incas used gold for their temple walls. The Khmers used reliefs and ornamentation literally wherever there was space for them, whereas the Incas' architecture was strictly functional. This, perhaps, was the resultant influence of the harsh alpine climate at high altitudes, and also because the buildings had to withstand frequent earthquakes. They had little time for stone friezes and statues, but their artistic expression was particularly developed by the goldsmiths, whose works of art were melted down into gold bars by those Spanish vandals, the Conquistadors.

One of the Inca building complexes also existed for a long time only as a legend, until in 1922 the American Senator Hiram Bingham found the "forgotten city" and proved that the legend was true.

These two cultured nations were overrun at about the same time by the Siamese and the Spanish respectively. The Khmers were conquered by the Siamese in 1432, and exactly one hundred years later the Incas were defeated by the Conquistadors.

The epic friezes of the Khmers also recall the splendid wall paintings in the tombs in the Valley of Kings, which tell of battles, feasts and everyday life in the land of the Pharaohs. They recall, too, the reliefs on the wonderful buildings of Rameses II at Abu Simbel. But the Egyptian friezes seem far more uniform and stylised and are often craft-work rather than art. There thousands of slaves only had to follow the instructions of the master—just as to-day the natives in Kenya and Uganda produce wooden figurines for tourists, those little dolls which are certainly hand-made, but which nevertheless look as though they were manufactured by machine. The Khmers, on the other hand, were individuals.

I managed to hire an elephant at quite a high charge to be taken out to Angkor Thom to the wall with the bas-reliefs showing the Khmer war elephants during an attack. Naturally it was my intention that the elephant should enliven my pictures of so many dead ruins. The result, however, was remarkable, for the little working elephant, which had never had to do more than drag timber down to the river, looked almost as though it were stuffed, when seen against the background of bas-reliefs. For the masterly sculptured war elephants of the Khmer artist projected so realistically from the stone wall as to give me a clear picture of the raiding expeditions in Cambodia a thousand years ago. These reliefs also bear witness to the nation's unique artistic sense, with their hundreds of gods, demi-gods, kings, sacred snakes and crowds of graceful temple dancing girls. There is even a circus depicted with clowns and tight-rope walkers.

One point, however, could be criticised. The artists who have created the pretty dancing girls have been unable to see the feet in true perspective, and these girls, otherwise so gracious, have been given what to our eyes are enormous feet. But who knows? Perhaps at that time it was fashionable to have big feet, just as it still is in the Babembe tribe in Africa. Or they may possibly have thought it artistically correct to emphasise and enlarge the feet, the position of which was of such great importance in the old epic dances depicting historic events or religious legends.

One of the best-known statues is "The Leprous King." For some time it was thought that this must have been one of Angkor's most important builders, but it has now been discovered from the inscriptions that this was not a king at all, but a judge in hell. Nor is there, in fact, anything leprous about him, apart from the algæ which cover his face and arms.

The French restoration work during the last hundred years has been a considerable achievement. Gradually they have cut back the forest and revealed buildings that have been hidden for hundreds of years by a forest canopy. However, two of the most remote temples have been left untouched as they would have collapsed had the stonework been freed from the tenacious arms of the jungle creepers. After the Khmers had abandoned these wonderful buildings, the jungle spread a thick green cover over the temples and palaces. Wherever there was the least crack or crevice between the stones, the jungle seeds and rootlets found an entry. In some places the walls have been completely overturned by the growth of the roots which have lifted, perhaps by only an eighth of an inch a year, massive stone blocks which were designed to remain in position for ever.

In many places the tree roots extend like snakes for thirty to sixty feet over stone walls and gravel paths in their search for a hole or crack that they can penetrate. They are as thick as a thigh—and the jungle's own version of the naga. Only the few stone blocks which were cemented with vegetable glue have resisted their attack. But the French have restored the buildings, reliefs and statues stone by stone.

In other places the banyan trees have found a foothold right on top of the ruins. These trees are popularly known as "cheese-trees," because their roots creep down over the ruins like an enormous flowing Camembert.

Perhaps the most impressive sight was at Preah Khan, where the French have deliberately allowed one ruin to continue the hopeless struggle against the jungle, which has so covered it that not a single stone would be seen from a helicopter.

At Ta Prohm, one of the many temple complexes, one enters in a greenish half-light. Overturned statues and blocks of stone are covered with a layer of green moss, so that they blend in with the forest floor. At one place in the middle of the paved roadway the stones have been torn apart, and a tree 150 feet high now grows where once the Khmer King rode on his gold-caparisoned elephant.

At one moment a dark shadow appeared through an opening in a ruined wall and startled both my native camera bearer and I. It was so gloomy and lonely that I would not have been surprised if this were a leopard. But when we cautiously crept forwards, there was no trace of leopard paw marks, but at the foot of an ancient time-ravaged Buddha were two sticks of incense and some lilac-grey orchids, as silent witnesses that the holiness of Angkor was not completely forgotten.

The incense sticks were still alight. Slowly they burnt down. The brown ash remained for a long time and then broke under its own weight. There was not a breath of air, and the thin smoke rose vertically up to the face of the Buddha. It seemed as though I was witnessing the last spark of a dead culture.

It struck me as symbolic that I should see this in front of a statue of Buddha. If the neighbouring countries had been seriously imbued with the gentle teaching of Buddha, the temples of the Khmers might still to-day have had their golden roofs shining in the sun and this culture might have reached far greater heights.

But now I yearned for places where men were still building gilded temples and pagodas ensheathed in gold. I was now ready to see the great Pagoda of Shwe Dagon at Rangoon, which I had promised the abbot in Loi Kaw should be the last port of call on my journey. My camera boy spoke little amongst the ruins, for we were much too moved by what we saw. Quietly we drove back along the narrow jungle paths. I was glad that I had chosen a rickshaw instead of a noisy motor-car.

We overtook the elephant that had been my super at the big wall relief. It, too, was taciturn and appeared wholly devout. But suddenly the silence was broken, and at the next turning there was a stall with a noisy transistor radio which shattered our devotion with the capital's latest pop tunes.

We allowed the owner to sell us some Coca-Cola on condition that he stopped the noise. He told us that business was quite good. This year's sales were double those of last, and he thought he could make a hundred per cent increase in each succeeding year. He maintained that good times were on the way.

CHAPTER XVI

Why Buddha Smiles

WHEN I arrived back in Burma I noticed that Rangoon was as wet as ever. The Strand Hotel smelt of damp and it was still not possible to walk dryshod in the streets.

The ships are moored at Rangoon's dripping-wet harbour on the Irrawaddy River. Twice a day, when the tide had travelled the thirty miles up river from the mouth, these ships swung round so that they pointed alternately upstream and downstream, like giant pendulums to mark the time in a place where time otherwise seemed to stand still.

A gang of harbour coolies had crept under a pile of teak on the quay to shelter from a shower, one of the many which encourage the growth of moss and help to dull the golden top of the Shwe Dagon Pagoda.

A betel-seller passed by; she was soaked to the skin, and her bare toes left deep but transitory tracks in the mud. This Burmese girl was not smoking a white cheroot and there were no flying-fish playing over the muddy Irrawaddy; the fine pattern made by the raindrops was broken by semi-decayed branches, refuse and other filth washed down by the current. How indeed would Kipling have shaped his romantic poem "The Road to Mandalay" if he had managed to visit Burma before writing it?

Before the swinging boats had measured off the next moment of eternity the tropical rain ceased, and the coolies and mechanical cranes continued to struggle with the heavy trunks of teak. This is the second stage in the handling of the timber, which has already been hauled out of the big forests in the north by teams of elephants. From Rangoon the teak will be sent on to the next port, perhaps San Francisco or Boston, Southampton, Hamburg or Copenhagen.

I walked away from the harbour, and my rickshaw coolie was immediately at my side, even though the place had several exits. As my guardian angel he was always there, whether I left the hotel during the midday siesta, when everybody else was asleep, or whether I turned up somewhere without prior warning. But of course I had also become part of his life; and although I must have woken him up out of his rainy season hibernation, he could take comfort in the thought that there would be plenty of opportunity for sleep when I had departed.

I was driven up to the north-western part of the city, a distance of four to five miles, which my coolie covered at a trot. Perhaps he thought privately that his passenger was slightly mad or at any rate eccentric in wanting to be taken such a long way in a primitive rickshaw. The drivers of the cycle-rickshaws were a little more frank in their comments, for they drove up alongside and tried to shanghai me. It was almost unheard of for a white man to ride in an ordinary rickshaw, and they regarded it as a personal insult.

But my coolie put his best foot forward. Downhill he made long hops like the famous Zulu rickshaws in Durban, but still had enough breath left to scold the other drivers. He could squeeze his narrow rickshaw through the crowd in places where the slightly broader cycle-rickshaws stuck fast, and eventually he managed to rid himself of all his competitors.

Now and again I could take a bearing on our goal, the slender spires of the Golden Pagoda, and check that we were keeping to the right course through the throng.

When we were overtaken by a squall I was carefully covered up in a pink plastic sheet. I was not clear whether this was friendly solicitude or merely that a good coolie finds it practical politics to do more for European passengers than his numerous competitors. Later when the weather allowed me to remove my covering we had reached a beautiful shady avenue of flamboyant trees, and at the end of it lay Shwe Dagon, looking even larger and more impressive than I had ever imagined.

Four streets of covered bazaars led up from each point of the compass to the cliff on which the pagoda stood. At its base one could leave one's shoes for a penny or so.

"Aren't you going to give me a ticket?" I asked.

"It is not necessary in your case," replied the cloakroom attendant, holding up my shoes in front of the other footwear left in his charge. I immediately saw why: my size elevens looked like violin cases alongside the Burmese shoes, most of which were in children's sizes.

At the entrance to the main staircase were two white monsters with bulging red eyes and open mouths, which showed their powerful tusks; these were centaurs, something between a dog and a lion. They were some eighteen feet high and were intended as a protection for the sacred place.

Shwe Dagon Pagoda is easily three times as high as the Round Tower in Copenhagen, and I believe it covers an area of ground almost as big as Trafalgar Square. It is ensheathed in real gold and surrounded by scores of other golden pagodas and hundreds of Buddhas.

Among the many Buddha statues at Shwe Dagon there are seven—named after the seven planets—which are particularly important from the astrological point of view. In theory you can give your flowers to any Buddha, but most people choose one under whose heavenly sign they were born.

Gaily clad men, women and children arrived, not only with flowers, but also with candles or a small bowl of rice for their chosen statue.

Now I understood them. I no longer thought it odd that they should offer rice to a Buddha that could not eat; none of these men and women would dream of asking for personal favours, and in front of the images they were thinking of Buddha's good deeds, and of how they could try to follow his example.

Suddenly I understood why here in the East spiritual values are more highly regarded than the worldly goods of the West. I understood why a father will spend time playing with his children and making himself comfortable at home, whilst foreign exporters and businessmen are angry because the Burmese are not sufficiently enthusiastic to develop the economy of their own country.

I understood that the Burmese has enough and is at peace, provided he is not hungry—and nobody starves in Burma to-day.

The enormous courtyard of Shwe Dagon Pagoda and its crowds can be compared to the scene in any big square in a European city. It was teeming with people, both locals and tourists, and even had pigeons, but the man selling peas was outshone by a little girl with yellow mimosa in her hair and a lilac dress, who looked enchanting against the golden pagodas.

It also brought to mind the market streets in southern Europe, for

Like giant Camemberts the "cheese trees" grow over the old Khmer architecture, smothering the buildings and artistic reliefs

A view of the temple courtyard of Shwe Dagon in Rangoon, where the pagodas
and stupas are covered with real gold-leaf. Most Burmese would prefer to save up
for a piece of gold-leaf the size of a postage stamp, rather than accumulate money
for their own benefit. It is a great day when the family is ready to visit the temple
and fix their gold on the pagoda

Above: Shwehlyaung, the reclining Buddha at Pegu, is 180 feet long and 45 feet high at the shoulders. *Below:* A sailing-boat on Lake Inle. The parasol is also used as a sail

right up the long covered steps which lead to the temple courtyard itself there were hundreds of little booths, where they sold carved Buddhas, jewellery and souvenirs, as well as flowers and wax candles. Behind the booths were the small workshops, where just as in the *sukhs* of North Africa, one could see the wares being made.

Gold leaf was the most fashionable thing you could buy in the streets of the bazaars, for most Buddhists have an ambition to stick a piece of gold leaf on the giant pagoda. One could meet individuals or whole families who came up to the pagoda with gold leaf, their faces beaming with pleasure. Obviously it was a great occasion for them. Perhaps they had been saving up and looking forward to this for six months or more.

It was interesting to compare this with our western ambitions—television, a noisy car and other technical marvels.

I passed through the covered streets and reached the courtyard of the temple, where there was not a single merchant.

Here on the Mount Olympus of Burma my thoughts went back to Ancient Greece. In this local Acropolis I could see modern versions of Socrates, Aristotle and Plato wandering around in pairs, deep in thought. Others sat among the columns of the many Buddha temples and read to the youths about the life of Buddha, or discussed his philosophy of life. There were also some who sat alone, in such deep meditation that they did not even blink if I used my camera tactlessly.

But unlike the ancient Greeks, who had a number of gods, the Burmese have Buddha as their sole model. Whereas the Greeks were helped by the gods of Olympus, the Buddhist has a greater personal responsibility, for he is complete master of his own destiny.

Together with U Ba Thaung, one of my friends from Loi Kaw, and his friend U Ral Hmung, I penetrated the gloom of one of the Buddhist temples. We sat leaning against the cool marble pillars and watched the world go by.

"Why do they pour water on to that Buddha?" I asked. For near to where we were sitting there was a steady stream of people going from a water tap up to one of the Buddhas. This little statue looked like all the others, except that it appeared to feel the need of a shower bath all the time.

"It is to obtain pardon and to wash away their sins," replied Thaung. Thaung was a Catholic, but his friend U Ral Hmung was a Buddhist.

U Ral Hmung spoke little English and was rather embarrassed about this. I could clearly see that he was not in complete agreement with Thaung, but he was too peaceful a man to contradict him.

"My dear friend," I said, "you are a Catholic, and as a Catholic you can obtain absolution, but you must know that a Buddhist may not pray for anything for himself, so I cannot accept your explanation."

At this point U Ral Hmung joined in the conversation, although rather diffidently.

"When we throw water over the Buddhas in Shwe Dagon it seems to us that we lighten our burden a little, because we can think about Buddha's good deeds at the same time."

But I never really understood why some Buddhas should be treated to a shower and others to wax candles. The ceremony corresponds to the Christian habit of putting flowers on a grave to show respect and veneration for the deceased.

In the cool shade of a quiet temple it was natural and obvious to talk about the philosophy of life, and the conversation now turned to the future. Thaung was a keen advocate of western civilisation and its spread.

"We under-developed countries are very behindhand in comparison with you," he said.

"Yes, but you have the spiritual values. You have time to enjoy your family, or a sunset, time to be happy and to laugh and smile."

"But we are poor," interjected Thaung.

"No, you are rich," I replied. "For you can afford to ignore the rat race. In our western world almost everything is measured in terms of money, and so we have less interest in the spiritual values, nor have we time to devote to them. I believe that *we* are under-developed, and that we have a lot to learn from you."

We were all very excited. Thaung maintained that progress must be speeded up, U Ral Hmung was content with things as they were, and I myself was afraid that if progress was too fast it might destroy much of the value in the so-called under-developed countries. Fortunately the close proximity of the temple cooled our enthusiasm.

But technical progress was Thaung's hobby, and he told a story from which we derived a moral:

"Once when I was out on a trip in the country with two European friends we met a poor Shan man, who was laboriously carrying a child on his shoulders, while his wife trudged along at his side, staggering under the weight of a large sack of rice. The Europeans and I decided to stop and offer them a lift. But they wouldn't hear of it.

"Yes," continued Thaung, "that's all there is to my story, but I can't refrain from thinking about why they refused. Now, you're used to dealing with primitive people," he said, turning to me. "What do you think was the reason?"

"Perhaps they were frightened of the car," I suggested.

"No, certainly not," asserted Thaung. "There was another reason."

"Perhaps they were afraid that they would have to make some return, and were so poor that they could not afford anything."

"No, that wasn't the reason either, although it's feasible."

"Was it simply because legs are there to be walked on that they refused to use this new-fangled method of transport?" I asked.

"Yes, you're more or less right. The reason they wouldn't come with us was purely and simply a dislike of anything new—a dislike of progress. They had lived for many generations without motor-cars, and had still been happy, so why should they have anything to do with these new inventions?"

"But what do you think is the moral of this story?" continued Thaung. "Would you agree with me that these peasants should have accepted our offer of a lift?"

"No," I replied. "People who are happy and content with their lot, as they were, are quite right to be sceptical about new things."

"You're wrong," replied Thaung. "These people were ignorant and primitive; for example they knew nothing about our country's biggest enemy, the Communists. Just think, they were happily living without suspecting any danger from the north."

"I am no advocate of sticking your head in the sand," I replied, "but I see no advantage in people living in fear, and I don't believe that their lives would be any happier if they had a constant feeling of insecurity."

"Surely ignorance can never be an excuse. But we shall be busy if we are to keep up with developments. Probably half of my compatriots will be living tucked away in the country and eating with their fingers, whilst the first rocket is landing on the moon." He said this with dismay in his voice.

"Well, so what?" I asked.

Thaung laughed and said:

"Maybe you're right—perhaps I would prefer to live in a primitive hut out in our beautiful green countryside, rather than on the moon."

"I have read about the advanced state of social welfare in Denmark,"
Thaung said after this. "In my country we have to work to care for
our parents and grandparents. This social welfare must leave you very
free."

"Yes, in Denmark we can work to earn money for ourselves, instead
of working for our parents and grandparents. You are a Burmese who
thinks along western lines and would like to have more money and
more progress at the cost of happiness and harmony. But I, who am a
European, regard the way in which most Burmese take their time to
appreciate spiritual values as something beneficial. And our friend with
the Buddha smile is Burmese and he certainly prefers the Burmese way
of life."

"He is happy," replied Thaung, "but I am unhappy. I live under
powerful pressures that fight against development, but I still want
progress for myself and for my people."

"By progress you mean economic, commercial development, don't
you?" I asked.

"Yes. I don't take my Catholicism very seriously, for in a way
I'm against religions, because they all counteract economic development."

U Ral Hmung was sitting with the smile of Buddha on his face.
It was difficult to get a word out of him, but when I spoke of the
happy people of Burma he smiled and nodded.

U Ral Hmung is one of the wealthiest businessmen in Rangoon. But
I had the impression that he had not done anything special to get there,
for as he sat dreaming in the shade of the Buddhist temple he was not
thinking about his ships sailing the seven seas. He was dreaming only
of going out into the country and sitting at the foot of a pagoda and
gazing out over the flat paddy-fields, where the buffaloes were sedately
drawing the ploughs.

Whenever even the slow-paced business life of Rangoon becomes too
hectic, U Ral Hmung fulfils his dream of peace and enters a monastery.
There he wears the saffron *tchingan* for a few weeks and devotes himself
to the spiritual life.

Our friend with the Buddha smile appeared to be happy; he was the
richest of us all, but not on account of his money, which he will probably
give away or use to build a Buddhist pagoda in about ten years' time.
He was the richest from the human point of view, for he felt no pressure

and was not interested in social climbing. He was at peace with himself, and happy to be alive—just like the smiling peasants labouring in the green paddy-fields.

Even the giraffe women, with their pride in the frightful neck rings, they too were happy for the same reason.

That is why Buddha smiles.

Epilogue

JUST AS this book was going to press newspaper reports confirmed that developments in Burma have occurred of which I saw no sign when I was there.

General Ne Win's revolutionary government is going to assume control of the greater part of the country's private trade and make Burma into a Socialist state on the Yugoslavian pattern.

The military government has already taken over all the banks, as well as the Burma Oil Company, and is gradually closing the net around the timber and rice-milling industries. After that it wants to control all home and foreign trade.

The democratic Minister for Trade, Aung Gyi, was forced to resign in February and deported to northern Burma. He was succeeded by Ba Nyein, a Communist, and several other Communists have been given influential positions.

Burma receives additional Communist influence from her giant neighbour China. In spite of border disputes, there is every reason to believe that Burma feels a close link with China. As explained earlier in this book, one reason for this is the Burmese dislike of the Indians. One of the few possibilities of joining up with an influential neighbour is to form an alliance with Communist China, from whom Burma is at the moment receiving significant backing. In addition China has lent several hundred experts, and this has meant that many western technicians have been ordered home.

The secluded Burmese people, not much interested in either politics or personal property, are the easiest possible raw material for a firm military government.

Years of unstable conditions have meant that foreign capital has been quickly withdrawn. But Burma is nevertheless a rich country—one of Asia's most fertile. If it manages to settle down under a relatively tolerant Communist régime, it may well be that Burma can look forward to a brighter and more peaceful future.

J.B.